W9-AJQ-153

HYMNS

MELODY LINE, CHORDS AND WORDS
FOR KEYBOARD • GUITAR • VOCAL

HAL•LEONARD

T 110555

ISBN 0-7935-7343-2

Visit Hal Leonard on the internet at http://www.halleonard.com

7777 W. BLUEMOUND RD. P.O. BOX 13819 MILWAUKEE, WI 53213

Welcome to the PAPERBACK SONGS SERIES

Do you play piano, guitar, electronic keyboard, sing or play any instrument for that matter? If so, this handy "pocket tune" book is for you.

The concise, one-line music notation consists of:

MELODY, WORDS & CHORD SYMBOLS

Whether strumming the chords on guitar, "faking" an arrangement on piano/keyboard or singing the words, these fake book style arrangements can be enjoyed at any experience level – hobbyist to professional.

The musical skills necessary to successfully use this book are minimal. If you play guitar and need some help with chords, a basic chord chart is included at the back of the book.

While playing and singing is the first thing that comes to mind when using this book, it can also serve as a compact, comprehensive reference guide.

However you choose to use this PAPERBACK SONGS SERIES book, by all means have fun!

CONTENTS

ABIDE WITH ME

words by
Henry F. Lyte, 1847

music by
W.H. Monk, 1861

1. A - bide with me; fast falls the e - ven - tide;
2. Swift to its close ebbs out life's lit - tle day;
3. I need thy pres - ence ev - ery pass - ing hour.
4. I fear no foe, with thee at hand to bless;
5. Hold thou thy cross be - fore my clos - ing eyes;

the dark-ness deep - ens; Lord, with me a - bide.
earth's joys grow dim; its glo - ries pass a - way;
What but thy grace can foil the tempt-er's power?
ills have no weight, and tears no bit - ter - ness.
shine through the gloom and point me to the skies.

When oth - er help - ers fail and com-forts flee,
change and de - cay in all a - round I see;
Who, like thy - self, my guide and stay can be?
Where is death's sting? Where, grave, thy vic - to - ry?
Heaven's morn-ing breaks, and earth's vain shad-ows flee;

Help of the help-less, O a - bide with me.
O Thou who chang-est not, a - bide with me.
Through cloud and sun-shine, Lord, a - bide with me.
I tri - umph still, if thou a - bide with me.
in life, in death, O Lord, a - bide with me.

AH, HOLY JESUS

words by
Johann Heermann, 1630
Trans. Robert Bridges, 1899
Alt. Psalter Hymnal, 1987

music by
Johann Cräer, 1640

1. Ah, ho - ly Je - sus, how have You of -
2. Who was the guilt - y? Who brought this up -
3. For me, dear Je - sus, was Your in - car -
4. There - fore, dear Je - sus, since I can - not

fend - ed, That mor - tal judg - ment has on You de -
on You? It is my trea - son, Lord, that has un -
na - tion, Your mor - tal sor - row, and Your life's ob -
pay You, I do a - dore You, and will ev - er

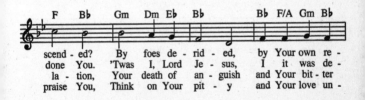

scend - ed? By foes de - rid - ed, by Your own re -
done You. 'Twas I, Lord Je - sus, I it was de -
la - tion, Your death of an - guish and Your bit - ter
praise You, Think on Your pit - y and Your love un -

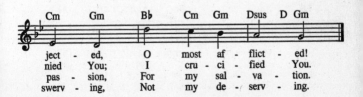

ject - ed, O most af - flict - ed!
nied You; I cru - ci - fied You.
pas - sion, For my sal - va - tion.
swerv - ing, Not my de - serv - ing.

ALAS, AND DID MY SAVIOR BLEED

words by
Isaac Watts, 1707

music by
Hugh Wilson, 1800
Adapt. and harm. Robert Smith, 1825

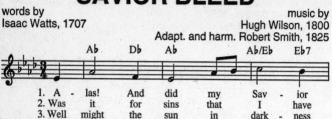

1. A - las! And did my Sav - ior
2. Was it for sins that I have
3. Well might the sun in dark - ness
4. But drops of grief can ne'er re -

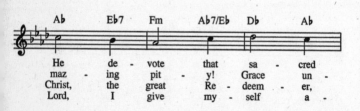

bleed, And did my Sov - ereign die! Would
done He suf - fered on the tree? A -
hide, And shut its glo - ries in, When
pay The debt of love I owe; Here,

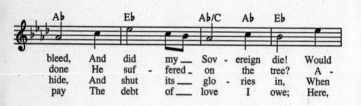

He de - vote that sa - cred
maz - ing pit - y! Grace un -
Christ, the great Re - deem - er,
Lord, I give my - self a -

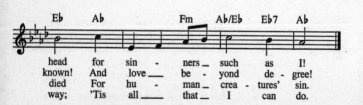

head for sin - ners such as I!
known! And love be - yond de - gree!
died For hu - man crea - tures' sin.
way; 'Tis all that I can do.

ALL GLORY, LAUD, AND HONOR

words by
Theodulph of Orleans, c. 820
Trans. John Mason Neale, 1851 1859

music by
Melchior Teschner, 1614
Arr. William Henry Monk, 1861

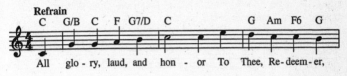

Refrain

All glo-ry, laud, and hon-or To Thee, Re-deem-er,

King! To whom the lips of chil-dren Made

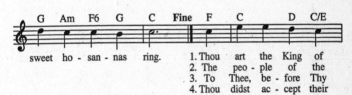

sweet ho-san-nas ring.

Fine

1. Thou art the King of
2. The peo-ple of the
3. To Thee, be-fore Thy
4. Thou didst ac-cept their

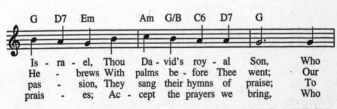

Is-ra-el, Thou Da-vid's roy-al Son, Who
He-brews With palms be-fore Thee went; Our
pas-sion, They sang their hymns of praise; To
prais-es; Ac-cept the prayers we bring, Who

Repeat Refrain

in the Lord's name com-est, The King and bless-ed One.
praise and prayers and an-thems Be-fore Thee we pre-sent.
Thee, now high ex-alt-ed, Our mel-o-dy we raise.
in all good de-light-est, Thou good and gra-cious King!

ALL CREATURES OF OUR GOD AND KING

words by
Francis of Assisi, 1225
Trans. and para.
William Henry Draper, c. 1910

music by
Geistliche Kirchengesäng, 1623
Harm. Ralph Vaughan Williams, 1906

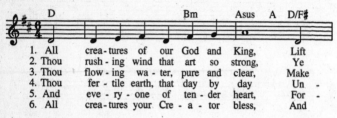

1. All   crea-tures of   our   God and   King,   Lift
2. Thou   rush-ing wind that art   so   strong,   Ye
3. Thou   flow-ing wa-ter, pure and   clear,   Make
4. Thou   fer-tile earth, that   day   by   day   Un-
5. And   eve-ry-one of   ten-der heart,   For-
6. All   crea-tures your Cre-a-tor bless,   And

up your voice and with us   sing,   Al-le-lu-ia!   Al-le-
clouds that sail in heaven a-long,   O __ sing ye!   Al-le-
mu-sic for thy Lord to   hear,   Al-le-lu-ia!   Al-le-
fold-est bless-ings on your way,   O __ sing ye!   Al-le-
giv-ing oth-ers, take your part.   O __ sing ye!   Al-le-
wor-ship God in hum-ble-ness.   O __ sing ye!   Al-le-

lu-ia! Thou   burn-ing sun with gold-en beam,   Thou
lu-ia! Thou   ris-ing morn, in praise re-joice,   Ye
lu-ia! Thou   fire so mas-ter-ful and bright,   That
lu-ia! The   flowers and fruits that in thee grow,   Let
lu-ia! Ye   who long pain and sor-row bear,   Praise
lu-ia! Praise, praise the Fa-ther, praise the Son,   And

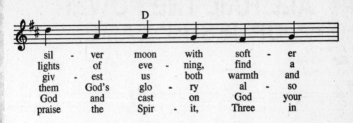

D

| sil - ver moon with soft - er |
| lights of eve - ning, find a |
| giv - est us both warmth and |
| them God's glo - ry al - so |
| praise the Spir - it, Three in |

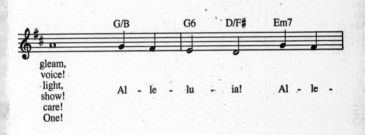

G/B   G6   D/F#   Em7

gleam,
voice!
light!   Al - le - lu - ia!   Al - le -
care!
One!

A7   Bm   E7   A   Bm

lu - ia!   Al - le - lu - ia!   Al - le -

Em   B/D#   Em   D/F#   G6   A7   D

lu - ia!   Al - le - lu - ia!

ALL HAIL THE POWER OF JESUS' NAME

words by
Edward Perronet, 1779
alt. by John Rippon, 1787

music by
Oliver Holden, 1792

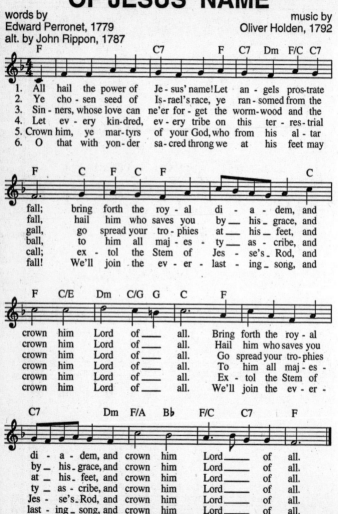

1. All hail the power of Je- sus' name! Let an- gels pros-trate
2. Ye cho- sen seed of Is- rael's race, ye ran- somed from the
3. Sin- ners, whose love can ne'er for- get the worm- wood and the
4. Let ev- ery kin- dred, ev- ery tribe on this ter- res- trial
5. Crown him, ye mar- tyrs of your God, who from his al- tar
6. O that with yon- der sa- cred throng we at his feet may

fall; bring forth the roy- al di - a - dem, and
fall, hail him who saves you by_ his_ grace, and
gall, go spread your tro- phies at_ his_ feet, and
ball, to him all maj- es- ty_ as- cribe, and
call; ex- tol the Stem of Jes- se's_ Rod, and
fall! We'll join the ev- er- last- ing_ song, and

crown him Lord of ___ all. Bring forth the roy- al
crown him Lord of ___ all. Hail him who saves you
crown him Lord of ___ all. Go spread your tro- phies
crown him Lord of ___ all. To him all maj- es-
crown him Lord of ___ all. Ex- tol the Stem of
crown him Lord of ___ all. We'll join the ev- er -

di - a - dem, and crown him Lord ___ of all.
by_ his_ grace, and crown him Lord ___ of all.
at_ his_ feet, and crown him Lord ___ of all.
ty_ as- cribe, and crown him Lord ___ of all.
Jes- se's_ Rod, and crown him Lord ___ of all.
last- ing_ song, and crown him Lord ___ of all.

ALL THINGS BRIGHT
AND BEAUTIFUL

words by
Cecil Frances Alexander,
1818–1895

music by
William Henry Monk, 1823–1889

ALLELUIA!

Traditional words   Traditional

1. Al - le - lu - ia,   Al - le - lu - ia,   Al - le -
2. He is ris - en,   Al - le - lu - ia,   He is
3. Je - sus loves me,   Al - le - lu - ia,   Je - sus
4. He is com - ing,   Al - le - lu - ia,   He is

lu - ia,   Al - le - lu - ia,   Al - le - lu - ia,   Al - le -
ris - en,   Al - le - lu - ia,   He is ris - en,   Al - le -
loves me,   Al - le - lu - ia,   Je - sus loves me,   Al - le -
com - ing,   Al - le - lu - ia,   He is com - ing,   Al - le -

lu - ia,   Al - le - lu - ia,
lu - ia,   He is ris - en,
lu - ia,   Je - sus loves me,   Praise the Lord!
lu - ia,   He is com - ing,

AM I A SOLDIER
OF THE CROSS

words by
Isaac Watts, *Sermons*, 1721-24
(1Cor. 16:13)

music by
Thomas A. Arne, 1762
Arr. by Ralph Harrison, 1784

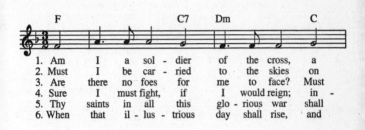

1. Am   I   a sol - dier   of the cross,   a
2. Must   I   be car - ried   to the skies   on
3. Are there no foes   for   me to face? Must
4. Sure   I   must fight, if   I would reign;   in -
5. Thy saints in all   this   glo - rious war   shall
6. When that il - lus - trious day shall rise,   and

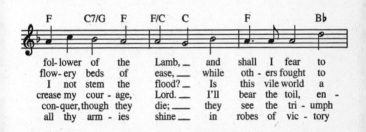

fol-lower of the   Lamb, _   and shall I fear   to
flow-ery beds of   ease, _   while oth - ers fought to
I   not stem the   flood? _   Is   this vile world a
crease my cour - age, Lord. _   I'll bear the toil, en -
con-quer, though they die; _   they see the tri - umph
all thy arm - ies   shine _   in   robes of vic - tory

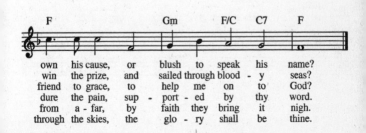

own   his cause,   or   blush to speak his   name?
win   the prize,   and sailed through blood - y seas?
friend to grace,   to   help   me   on   to   God?
dure the pain, sup - port - ed by thy word.
from a - far,   by   faith they bring it   nigh.
through the skies, the glo - ry shall be   thine.

AMAZING GRACE

words by
John Newton
John P. Rees, stanza 5

music by
Virginia Harmony, 1831
Arr. Edwin O. Excell

1. A - maz - ing __ grace! How sweet the
2. 'Twas grace that __ taught my heart to
3. Through man - y __ dan - gers, toils, and
4. The Lord has __ prom - ised good to
5. Yea, when this __ flesh and heart shall
6. When we've been __ there ten thou - sand

sound that saved a wretch like me! I
fear, and grace my fears re - lieved; how
snares, I have al - read - y come; 'tis
me, his word my hope se - cures; he
fail, and mor - tal life shall cease, I
years, bright shin - ing as the sun, we've

once __ was lost, but now __ am __
pre - cious did that grace __ ap -
grace hath __ brought me safe __ thus __
will __ my __ shield and por - tion __
shall __ pos - sess, with - in the __
no __ less __ days to sing __ God's _

found; was blind, but __ now I see.
pear the hour I __ first be - lieved.
far, and grace will __ lead me home.
be, as long as __ life en - dures.
veil, a life of __ joy and peace.
praise than when we'd __ first be - gun.

AND CAN IT BE
THAT I SHOULD GAIN

words by
Charles Wesley

music by
Thomas Campbell

1. And can it be that I should gain an in-t'rest in the Sav-ior's blood? Died He for me, who caused His pain? For me, who Him to death pur-sued? A-maz-ing love! how can it be That Thou, my God shouldst die for me?

2. He left His Fa-ther's throne a-bove, So free, so in-fi-nite His grace! Emp-tied Him-self of all but love, And bled for Ad-am's help-less race! 'Tis mer-cy all, im-mense and free, For, O my God, it found out me.

3. Long my im-pris-oned spir-it lay Fast bound in sin and na-ture's night. Thine eye dif-fused a quick-'ning ray: I woke the dun-geon flamed with light! My chains fell off, my heart was free, I rose, went forth, and fol-lowed Thee.

4. No con-dem-na-tion now I dread: Je-sus, and all in Him, is mine! A-live in Him my liv-ing Head, And clothed in right-eous-ness di-vine, Bold I ap-proach th'e-ter-nal throne, And claim the crown, thee Christ my own.

Refrain

A-maz-ing love! how can it be That Thou, my God, shouldst die for me!

ASK YE WHAT GREAT THING I KNOW

words by
Johann C. Schwedler, 1741
trans. by Benjamin H. Kennedy, 1863
(1 Cor. 2:2; Gal. 6:14)

music by
H.A. César Malan, 1827
Harm. by Lowell Mason, 1841

1. Ask ye what great thing I know,
that delights and stirs me so?
What the high reward I win?
Whose the name I glory in?
Jesus Christ, the crucified.

2. Who defeats my fiercest foes?
Who consoles my saddest woes?
Who revives my fainting heart,
healing all its hidden smart?
Jesus Christ, the crucified.

3. Who is life in life to me?
Who the death of death will be?
Who will place me on his right,
with the countless hosts of light?
Jesus Christ, the crucified.

4. This is that great thing I know;
this delights and stirs me so:
faith in him who died to save,
him who triumphed o'er the grave:
Jesus Christ, the crucified.

AWAKE, AWAKE
TO LOVE AND WORK

words by
Geoffrey Anketel Studdert-Kennedy
(1883–1929)

music by
Morning Song, melody att.
harm. Charles Winfred Douglas
(1867–1944)

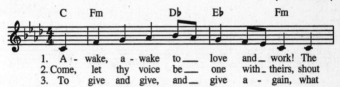

1. A- wake, a- wake to love and work! The
2. Come, let thy voice be one with theirs, shout
3. To give and give, and give a - gain, what

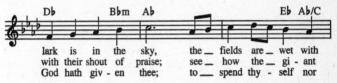

lark is in the sky, the fields are wet with
with their shout of praise; see how the gi- ant
God hath giv- en thee; to spend thy- self nor

dia- mond dew, the worlds a- wake to
sun soars up, great lord of years and
count the cost; to serve right glo- rious-

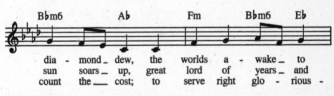

cry their bless- ings on the
days! So let the love of
ly the God who gave all

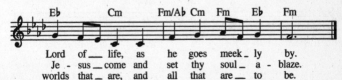

Lord of life, as he goes meek ly by.
Je- sus come and set thy soul a- blaze.
worlds that are, and all that are to be.

BE PRESENT
AT OUR TABLE

words by
John Cennick, 1741, alt.

music by
Attr. to Louis Bourgeois, 1551

Be pres - ent at our ta - ble, Lord; be

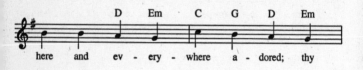

here and ev - ery - where a - dored; thy

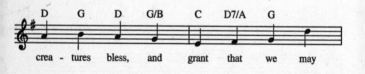

crea - tures bless, and grant that we may

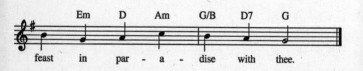

feast in par - a - dise with thee.

BE THOU MY VISION

words by
Ancient Irish poem
Trans. Mary E. Byrne, 1905
Vers. Eleanor Hull, 1912

music by
Irish ballad
Harm. David Evans, 1927

1. Be Thou my vi - sion, O Lord of my heart;
2. Rich - es I heed not, nor vain, emp - ty praise.
3. Be Thou my wis - dom, and Thou my true word;
4. High King of hea - ven, when vic - to - ry is won,

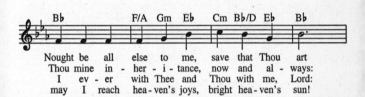

Nought be all else to me, save that Thou art
Thou mine in - her - i - tance, now and al - ways:
I ev - er with Thee and Thou with me, Lord:
may I reach hea - ven's joys, bright hea - ven's sun!

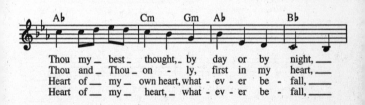

Thou my best thought, by day or by night,
Thou and Thou on - ly, first in my heart,
Heart of my own heart, what - ev - er be - fall,
Heart of my heart, what - ev - er be - fall,

Wak - ing or sleep - ing, Thy pres - ence my light.
Great God of heav - en, my trea - sure Thou art.
Still be my vi - sion, O Rul - er of all.
Still be my vi - sion, O Rul - er of all.

THE BEAUTIFUL GARDEN OF PRAYER

words by
Eleanor Allen Schroll

music by
James H. Fillmore 1849–1936

1. There's a gar - den where Je - sus is
2. There's a gar - den where Je - sus is
3. There's a gar - den where Je - sus is

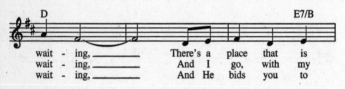

wait - ing, _____ There's a place that is
wait - ing, _____ And I go, with my
wait - ing, _____ And He bids you to

won - drous - ly fair, _____ For it
bur - den and care, _____ Just to
come meet Him there, _____ Just to

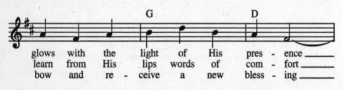

glows with the light of His pres - ence _____
learn from His lips words of com - fort _____
bow and re - ceive a new bless - ing _____

_____ 'Tis the beau - ti - ful gar - den of
_____ In the beau - ti - ful gar - den of
_____ In the beau - ti - ful gar - den of

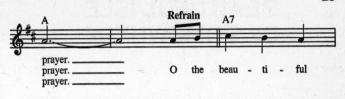

prayer. _____
prayer. _____
prayer. _____ O the beau - ti - ful

gar - den, the gar - den of prayer, O the

beau - ti - ful gar - den of prayer! _____

_____ There my Sav - ior a - waits, and He

o - pens the gates To the beau - ti - ful

gar - den of prayer. _____

BEAUTIFUL ISLE
OF SOMEWHERE

words by
Jessie B. Pounds, 1861–1921

music by
J.S. Fearis

1. Some-where the sun is shin - ing,
2. Some-where the day is lon - ger,
3. Some-where the load is lift - ed,

Some-where the song - birds dwell; _____
Some-where the task is done; _____
Close by an o - pen gate; _____

Hush, then, thy sad re - pin - ing,
Some-where the heart is stron - ger,
Some-where the clouds are rift - ed,

God lives, and all is well. _____
Some-where the guer - don won. _____
Some-where the an - gels wait. _____

Refrain

Some-where, some-where, Beau-ti-ful is-le of

some - where; Land of the true, where we

live a-new, Beau-ti-ful is-le of some - where.

BEAUTIFUL SAVIOR

music by
Gesangbuch, *Münster*, 1677
tr. Joseph A. Seiss, 1823–1904

music by
Silesian folk tune, 1842

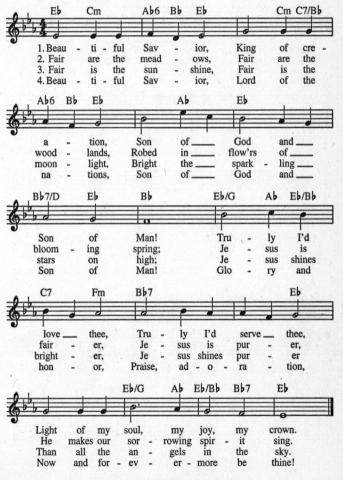

1. Beau - ti - ful Sav - ior, King of cre - a - tion, Son of ___ God and ___ Son of Man! Tru - ly I'd love ___ thee, Tru - ly I'd serve ___ thee, Light of my soul, my joy, my crown.
2. Fair are the mead - ows, Fair are the wood - lands, Robed in ___ flow'rs of ___ bloom - ing spring; Je - sus is fair - er, Je - sus is pur - er, He makes our sor - rowing spir - it sing.
3. Fair is the sun - shine, Fair is the moon - light, Bright the ___ spark - ling stars on high; Je - sus shines bright - er, Je - sus shines pur - er Than all the an - gels in the sky.
4. Beau - ti - ful Sav - ior, Lord of the na - tions, Son of ___ God and ___ Son of Man! Glo - ry and hon - or, Praise, ad - o - ra - tion, Now and for - ev - er - more be thine!

BEFORE THE LORD JEHOVAH'S THRONE

words by
Isaac Watts, 1719
based on Psalm 100

music by
Frederic Venua

1. Be - fore the Lord ___ Je - ho - vah's
2. His sov - ereign power, ___ with - out ___ our
3. We'll crowd his gates ___ with thank - ful
4. Wide as the world ___ is his ___ com -

throne, All na - tions bow ___ with
aid, Made us of clay, ___ and
songs, High as the heavens ___ our
mand, Vast as e - ter - ni -

sa - cred joy; Know that the Lord is
formed us men; And when like wan - d'ring
voic - es raise; And earth, with her ten
ty his love; Firm as a rock his

God a - lone, He can cre - ate, and
sheep we strayed, He brought us to his
thou - sand tongues, Shall fill his courts with
truth shall stand, When roll - ing years shall

he de - stroy. He can cre -
fold a - gain. He brought us
sound - ing praise. Shall fill his
cease to move. When roll - ing

ate, and he de - stroy.
to his fold a - gain.
courts with sound - ing praise.
years shall cease to move.

BENEATH THE CROSS
OF JESUS

words by
Elizabeth Cecilia Douglas Clephane,
1868

music by
Frederick Charles Maker,
1881

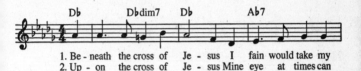

1. Be - neath the cross of Je - sus I fain would take my
2. Up - on the cross of Je - sus Mine eye at times can

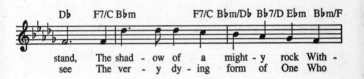

stand, The shad - ow of a might - y rock With -
see The ver - y dy - ing form of One Who

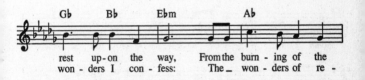

in a wea - ry land; A home with - in the wil - der - ness, A
suf - fered there for me: And from my strick - en heart with tears Two

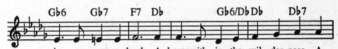

rest up - on the way, From the burn - ing of the
won - ders I con - fess: The _ won - ders of re -

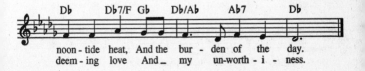

noon - tide heat, And the bur - den of the day.
deem - ing love And _ my un - worth - i - ness.

BEULAH LAND

words by
Edgar Page

music by
Jno. R. Sweney

1. I've reached the land of corn and wine, And all its rich-es free-ly mine; Here shines un-dimmed one bliss-ful day, For all my night has passed a-way.
2. My Sav-ior comes and walks with me, And sweet com-mu-ion here have we; He gen-tly leads me by His hand For this is heav-en's bor-der-land.
3. A sweet per-fume up-on the breeze Is born from ev-er-ver-nal trees, And flow'rs,that nev-er-fad-ing grow Where streams of life for-ev-er flow;
4. The zeph-yrs seem to float to me Sweet sounds of heav-en's mel-o-dy, As an-gels with the-white-robed throng Join in the sweet re-demp-tion song.

Chorus

Beu-lah Land, sweet Beu-lah Land, As on thy high-est mount I stand, I look a-way a-cross the sea, Where man-sions are pre-pared for me, And view the shin-ing glo-ry-shore My heav'n, my home for-ev-er more!

BLESSED ASSURANCE

Words:
Fanny J. Crosby, 1873

music by
Phoebe P. Knapp, 1873

1. Bless-ed as - sur - ance, Je - sus is mine! __ O what a fore - taste of glo - ry di - vine! __ Heir of sal - va - tion, pur-chase of God, __ born of his Spir - it, washed in his blood. __ This is my sto - ry, this is my song, __ prais-ing my Sav - ior all the day long; __ this is my sto - ry, this is my song, __ prais-ing my Sav - ior all the day long. __

2. Per-fect sub - mis - sion, per-fect de - light, __ vi-sions of rap - ture now burst on my sight; __ an - gels de - scend-ing bring from a - bove __ ech - oes of mer - cy, whis-pers of love. __

3. Perfect sub-mis - sion, all is at rest; __ I in my Sav - ior am hap - py and blest, __ watch-ing and wait - ing, look-ing a - bove, __ filled with his good-ness, lost in his love. __

BLEST BE THE TIE
THAT BINDS

words by
John Fawcett, 1782

music by
Johann G. Nägeli
arr. by Lowell Mason, 1845

1. Blest be the tie that binds our
2. Be fore our Fa ther's throne we
3. We share each oth er's woes, our
4. When we a sun der part, it

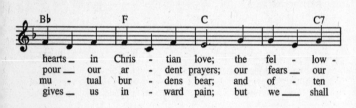

hearts in Chris tian love; the fel low -
pour our ar dent prayers; our fears our
mu tual bur dens bear; and of ten
gives us in ward pain; but we shall

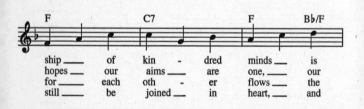

ship of kin dred minds is
hopes our aims are one, our
for each oth er flows the
still be joined in heart, and

like to that a bove.
com forts and our cares.
sym pa thiz ing tear.
hope to meet a gain.

BREAD OF THE WORLD

words by
Reginald Heber (1783–1826)

music by
Rendez à Dieu, melody att.
Louis Bourgeois (1510-1561)
harm. Claude Goudimel (1541–1572), alt.

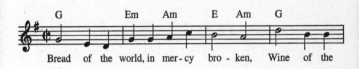

Bread of the world, in mer - cy bro - ken, Wine of the

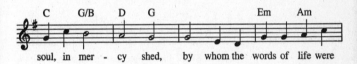

soul, in mer - cy shed, by whom the words of life were

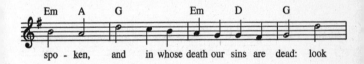

spo - ken, and in whose death our sins are dead: look

on the heart by sor - row bro - ken, look on the

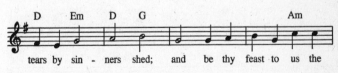

tears by sin - ners shed; and be thy feast to us the

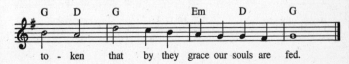

to - ken that by they grace our souls are fed.

BREAK THOU THE
BREAD OF LIFE

words by
Mary Artemesia Lathbury, 1877

music by
William Fiske Sherwin, 1877

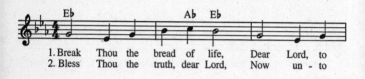

1. Break Thou the bread of life, Dear Lord, to
2. Bless Thou the truth, dear Lord, Now un - to

me, As Thou didst break the loaves Be -
me, As Thou didst bless the bread By

side the sea; Be - yond the
Gal - i - lee; Then shall all

sa - cred page I seek Thee, Lord;
bond - age cease, All fet - ters fall;

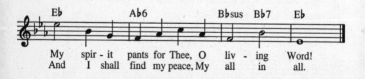

My spir - it pants for Thee, O liv - ing Word!
And I shall find my peace, My all in all.

BREATHE ON ME, BREATH OF GOD

words by
Edwin Hatch, 1886

music by
Robert Jackson, 1894

1. Breathe on me, Breath of God,
2. Breathe on me, Breath of God,
3. Breathe on me, Breath of God,
4. Breathe on me, Breath of God,

Fill me with life a - new,
Un - til my heart is pure,
Till I am whol - ly Thine,
So shall I nev - er die,

That I may love what Thou dost
Un - til with Thee I will one
Un - til this earth - ly part of
But live with Thee the per - fect

love, And do ____ what Thou wouldst do.
will, To do ____ and to en - dure.
me Glows with ____ Thy fire di - vine.
life Of Thine ____ e - ter - ni - ty.*

*Repeat stanza 1.

BRINGING IN THE SHEAVES

words by
Knowles Shaw, 1834–1878

music by
George A. Minor

1. Sow-ing in the morn-ing, sow-ing seeds of kind-ness,
2. Sow-ing in the sun-shine, sow-ing in the shad-ows,
3. Go-ing forth with weep-ing, sow-ing for the Mas-ter,

Sow-ing in the noon-tide and the dew-y eve;
Fear-ing nei-ther clouds nor win-ter's chill-ing breeze;
Though the loss sus-tained our spir-it of-ten grieves;

Wait-ing for the har-vest, and the time of reap-ing,
By and by the har-vest, and the la-bor end-ed,
When our weep-ing's o-ver, He will bid us wel-come,

We shall come re-joic-ing, bring-ing in the sheaves.
We shall come re-joic-ing, bring-ing in the sheaves.
We shall come re-joic-ing, bring-ing in the sheaves.

Refrain

Bring-ing in the sheaves, Bring-ing in the sheaves,

1.
We shall come re-joic-ing bring-ing in the sheaves.

2.
bring-ing in the sheaves.

A CHARGE TO KEEP I HAVE

words by
Charles Wesley

music by
Lowell Mason

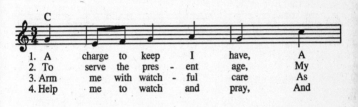

1. A charge to keep I have, A
2. To serve the pres - ent age, My
3. Arm me with watch - ful care As
4. Help me to watch and pray, And

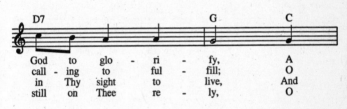

God to glo - ri - fy, A
call - ing to ful - fill; O
in Thy sight to live, And
still on Thee re - ly, O

nev - er - dy - ing soul to save, And
may it all my pow'rs en - gage To
now Thy ser - vant, Lord, pre - pare A
let me not my trust be - tray, But

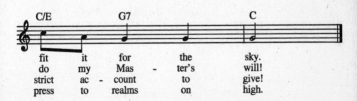

fit it for the sky.
do my Mas - ter's will!
strict ac - count to give!
press to realms on high.

BUILT ON THE ROCK

words by
Nicolai F.S. Grundtvig, 1837

Music:
Ludvig M. Lindeman, 1840
Trans. Carl Döving, 1909, 1972

1. Built on the rock the church does stand, Even when steeples are fall - ing; Crumbled have spires in ev - ery land,
2. Sure - ly in tem - ples made with hands, God, the most high, is not dwell - ing; High a - bove earth his tem - ple stands,
3. We are God's house of liv - ing stones, Build - ed for his habi - ta - tion; He through bap - tis - mal grace us owns,
4. Now we may gath - er with our Kings, E'en in the low - li - est dwell - ing; Prais - es to him we there may bring,

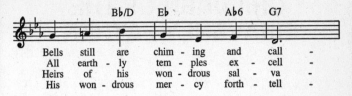

Bb/D	Eb		Ab6	G7

Bells still are chim - ing and call -
All earth - ly tem - ples ex - cell -
Heirs of his won - drous sal - va -
His won - drous mer - cy forth - tell -

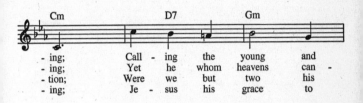

Cm	D7	Gm

- ing; Call - ing the young and
- ing; Yet he whom heavens can -
- tion; Were we but two his
- ing; Je - sus his grace to

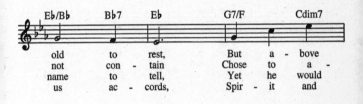

Eb/Bb	Bb7	Eb	G7/F	Cdim7

old to rest, But a - bove
not con - tain Chose to a -
name to tell, Yet he would
us ac - cords, Spir - it and

Gm/Bb	Cm6	Gm/D	D7	Gm

all the soul dis - tressed,
bide on earth with men,
deign with us to dwell,
life are all his words,

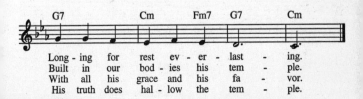

G7	Cm	Fm7	G7	Cm

Long - ing for rest ev - er - last - ing.
Built in our bod - ies his tem - ple.
With all his grace and his fa - vor.
His truth does hal - low the tem - ple.

CHILDREN OF THE HEAVENLY FATHER

words by
Simon Browne, 1680–1732, alt.

music by
William Knapp, 1698–1768

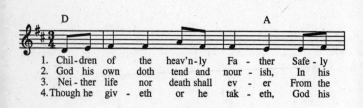

1. Chil-dren of the heav'n-ly Fa-ther Safe-ly
2. God his own doth tend and nour-ish, In his
3. Nei-ther life nor death shall ev-er From the
4. Though he giv-eth or he tak-eth, God his

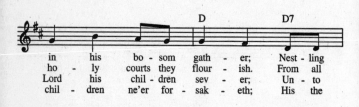

in his bo-som gath-er; Nest-ling
ho-ly courts they flour-ish. From all
Lord his chil-dren sev-er; Un-to
chil-dren ne'er for-sak-eth; His the

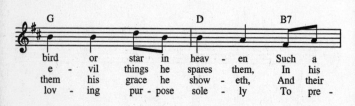

bird or star in heav-en Such a
e-vil things he spares them, In his
them his grace he show-eth, And their
lov-ing pur-pose sole-ly To pre-

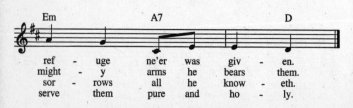

ref-uge ne'er was giv-en.
might-y arms he bears them.
sor-rows all he know-eth.
serve them pure and ho-ly.

CHRIST AROSE

words by
Robert Lowry

music by
Robert Lowry

1. Low in the grave He lay, Je - sus my Sav - ior! Wait - ing the com - ing day, Je - sus my Lord!
2. Vain - ly they watch His bed, Je - sus my Sav - ior! Vain - ly they seal the dead,
3. Death can - not keep his prey, Je - sus my Sav - ior! He tore the bars a - way,

Refrain

Up from the grave He a - rose, With a might - y tri - umph o'er His foes; He a - rose a Vic - tor from the dark do - main, And He lives for - ev - er with His saints to reign, He a - rose! He a - rose! Hal - le - lu - jah! Christ a - rose!

CHRIST THE LORD IS RISEN TODAY

words by
Charles Wesley, 1739

music by
from *Lyra Davidica*, London, 1708

1. Christ the Lord is risen to-day, ___ Al - le - lu - ia! Earth and heaven in cho - rus say, __ Al - le - lu - ia! Raise your joys and tri - umphs high, Al - le - lu - ia! Sing, __ ye __ heavens, and earth re - ply, __ Al - le - lu - ia!

2. Love's re - deem - ing work is done, ___ Al - le - lu - ia! Fought the fight, the bat - tle won, __ Al - le - lu - ia! Death in vain for - bids him, rise, Al - le - lu - ia! Christ, __ has __ o - pened par - a - dise, __ Al - le - lu - ia!

3. Lives a - gain our glo - rious King, ___ Al - le - lu - ia! Where, O death, is now thy sting? __ Al - le - lu - ia! Once he died our souls to save, Al - le - lu - ia! Where's __ the __ vic - tory, boast - ing grave? __ Al - le - lu - ia!

4. Soar we now where Christ has led, ___ Al - le - lu - ia! Fol - lowing our ex - alt - ed Head, Al - le - lu - ia! Made like him, like him we rise, Al - le - lu - ia! Ours __ the __ cross, the grave, the skies, __ Al - le - lu - ia!

CHRIST, WHOSE GLORY FILLS THE SKIES

words by
Charles Wesley, 1740

German melody
adapted in Werner's *Choralbuch*, 1815

1. Christ, whose glo - ry fills the skies,
2. Dark and cheer - less is the morn,
3. Vis - it, then, this soul of mine;

Christ, the true, the on - ly light,
Un - ac - com - pa - nied by thee;
Pierce the gloom of sin and grief;

Sun of righ - teous - ness, a - rise,
Joy - less is the day's re - turn,
Fill me, Ra - dian - cy di - vine,

Tri - umph o'er the shades of night;
Till they mer - cy's beams I see,
Scat - ter all my un - be - lief;

Day - spring from on high, be near;
Till they in - ward light im - part,
More and more thy - self dis - play,

Day - star, in my heart ap - pear.
Glad my eyes and warm my heart.
Shin - ing to the per - fect day.

THE CHURCH'S ONE FOUNDATION

words by
Samuel John Stone
(1839–1900)

music by
Aurelia, Samuel Sebastian Wesley
(1810–1876)

1. The church's one foun- da- tion is Je- sus Christ her Lord; she is his new cre- a- tion by wa- ter and the word: from heaven he came and sought her to be his ho- ly bride; with his own blood he bought her, and for her life he died.

2. E- lect from ev- ery na- tion, yet one o'er all the earth, her char- ter of sal- va- tion, one Lord, one faith, one birth; one ho- ly Name she bless- es, par- takes one ho- ly food, and to one hope she press- es, with ev- ery grace en- dued.

3. Though with a scorn- ful won- der men see her sore op- pressed, by schi- sms rent a- sun- der, by her- e- sies dis- tressed; yet saints their watch are keep- ing, their cry goes up, "How long?" and soon the night of weep- ing shall be the morn of song.

4. Mid toil and tri- bu- la- tion, and tu- mult of her war she waits the con- sum- ma- tion of peace for ev- er- more; till with the vi- sion glo- rious her long- ing eyes are blessed, and the great Church vic- to- rious shall be the Church at rest.

5. Yet she on earth hath un- ion with God, the Three in One, and mys- tic sweet com- mun- ion with those whose rest is won. O hap- py ones and ho- ly! Lord, give us grace that we like them, the meek and low- ly, on high may dwell with thee.

CLOSE TO THEE

words by
Fanny J. Crosby

music by
Silas J. Vail

1. Thou, my ev - er - last - ing por - tion, More than friend or life to me, All a - long my pil - grim jour - ney, Sav - ior, let me walk with Thee. Close to Thee, close to Thee, Close to Thee, close to Thee; All a - long my pil - grim jour - ney, Sav - ior, let me walk with Thee.

2. Not for ease or world - ly pleas - ure Nor for fame my prayer shall be; Glad - ly will I toil and suf - fer, On - ly let me walk with Thee. Close to Thee, close to Thee, Close to Thee, close to Thee; Glad - ly will I toil and suf - fer, On - ly let me walk with Thee.

3. Lead me thru the vale of shad - ows, Bear me o'er life's fit - ful sea; Then the gate of life e - ter - nal May I en - ter, Lord, with Thee. Close to Thee, close to Thee, Close to Thee, close to Thee; Then the gate of life e - ter - nal May I en - ter, Lord, with Thee.

COME, THOU ALMIGHTY KING

words by
source unknown, c. 1757, alt.

music by
Felice de Giardini, 1716–1796

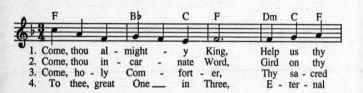

1. Come, thou al-might-y King, Help us thy
2. Come, thou in-car-nate Word, Gird on thy
3. Come, ho-ly Com-fort-er, Thy sa-cred
4. To thee, great One in Three, E-ter-nal

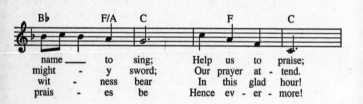

name to sing; Help us to praise;
might-y sword; Our prayer at-tend.
wit-ness bear In this glad hour!
prais-es be Hence ev-er-more!

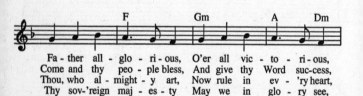

Fa-ther all-glo-ri-ous, O'er all vic-to-ri-ous,
Come and thy peo-ple bless, And give thy Word suc-cess,
Thou, who al-might-y art, Now rule in ev-'ry heart,
Thy sov-'reign maj-es-ty May we in glo-ry see,

Come and reign o-ver us, An-cient of Days.
And let thy righ-teous-ness On us de-scend.
And ne'er from us de-part, Spir-it of pow'r.
And to e-ter-ni-ty Love and a-dore.

COME, THOU FOUNT
OF EVERY BLESSING

words by
Robert Robinson, 1758
(1 Sam. 7:12)

music by
Wyeth's *Repository of Sacred Music,*
Part Second, 1813

1. Come, thou Fount of ev-ery bless-ing, tune my
2. Here I raise mine Eb-e-ne-zer; hith-er
3. O to grace how great a debt-or dai-ly

heart to sing thy grace; streams of mer-cy, nev-er
by thy help I'm come; and I hope, by thy good
I'm con-strained to be! Let thy good-ness, like a

ceas-ing, call for songs of loud-est praise. Teach me
plea-sure, safe-ly to ar-rive at home. Je-sus
fet-ter, bind my wan-dering heart to thee. Prone to

some me-lo-dious son-net, sung by
sought me when a stran-ger, wan-dering
wan-der, Lord, I feel it, prone to

flam-ing tongues a-bove. Praise the mount! I'm fixed up-
from the fold of God; he, to res-cue me from
leave the God I love; here's my heart, O take and

on it, mount of thy re-deem-ing love.
dan-ger, in-ter-posed his pre-cious blood.
seal it, seal it for thy courts a-bove.

COME YE FAITHFUL, RAISE THE STRAIN

words by
John of Damascus (8th cent.)
tr. John Mason Neale
(1818–1866), alt.

music by
St. Kevin, Arthur Seymour Sullivan
(1842–1900)

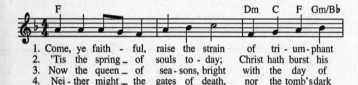

1. Come, ye faith - ful, raise the strain of tri - um - phant
2. 'Tis the spring _ of souls to - day; Christ hath burst his
3. Now the queen _ of sea - sons, bright with the day of
4. Nei - ther might _ the gates of death, nor the tomb's dark

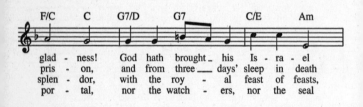

glad - ness! God hath brought _ his Is - ra - el
pris - on, and from three ___ days' sleep in death
splen - dor, with the roy - al feast of feasts,
por - tal, nor the watch - ers, nor the seal

in - to joy from _ sad - ness: loosed from Pha - roah's
as a sun hath _ ris - en; all the win - ter
comes its joy to _ ren - der; comes to glad _ Je -
hold thee as a ___ mor - tal: but to - day _ a -

49

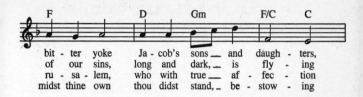

bit - ter yoke   Ja - cob's   sons __ and   daugh - ters,
of   our   sins,   long   and   dark, __ is   fly - ing
ru - sa - lem,   who with   true __ af - fec - tion
midst thine own   thou didst   stand, __ be - stow - ing

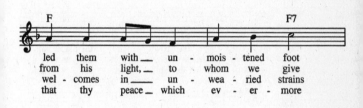

led   them   with __   un - mois - tened   foot
from   his   light, __   to   whom   we   give
wel - comes   in __   un - wea - ried   strains
that   thy   peace __   which   ev - er - more

through   the   Red   Sea   wa - ters.
laud   and   praise   un - dy - ing.
Je - sus'   re - sur - rec - tion.
pass - eth   hu - man   know - ing.

COME, YE THANKFUL PEOPLE, COME

words by
Henry Alford (1810–1871), *St. George's, Windsor,* George Job Elvey
alt.   (1816–1893)

desc. Craig Sellar Lang (1891-1971)

1. Come, ye thank-ful peo-ple, come, raise the song of
2. All the world is God's own field, fruit un-to his
3. For the Lord our God shall come, and shall take his
4. E- ven so, Lord, quick-ly come to thy fi-nal

har-vest-home: all is safe-ly gath-ered in,
praise to yield; wheat and tares to-geth-er sown,
har-vest-home; from his field shall in that day
har-vest-home; gath-er thou thy peo-ple in,

ere the win-ter storms be-gin; God, our Ma-ker,
un-to joy or sor-row grown: first the blade, and
all of-fens-es purge a-way; give his an-gels
free from sor-row, free from sin; there, for ev-er

doth pro-vide for our wants to be sup-plied;
then the ear, then the full corn shall ap-pear:
change at last in the fire the tares to cast,
pur-i-fied, in thy pres-ence to a-bide;

come to God's own tem-ple, come,
grant, O har-vest Lord, that we
but the fruit-ful ears to store
come, with all thine an-gels come,

raise the song of har-vest-home.
whole-some grain and pure may be.
in his gar-ner ev-er-more.
raise the glo-rious har-vest-home.

CROWN HIM
WITH MANY CROWNS

words by
Matthew Bridges
(1800–1894)

music by
Diademata, George Job Elvey (1816–1893)
desc. Richard Proulx (b. 1937)

1. Crown him with man-y crowns, the Lamb up-on his throne; Hark! how the heaven-ly an-them drowns all mu-sic but its own; a-wake, my soul, and sing of him who died for thee, and hail him as thy match-less King through all e-ter-ni-ty.

2. Crown him the son of God be-fore the worlds be-gan, and ye, who tread where he hath trod, crown him the Son of man; who ev-ery grief hath known that wrings the hu-man breast, and takes and bears them for his own, that all in him may rest.

3. Crown him the Lord of life, who tri-umphed o'er the grave, and rose vic-to-rious in the strife for those he came to save; his glo-ries now we sing who died, and rose on high, who died, e-ter-nal life to bring, and lives that death may die.

4. Crown him of lords the Lord, who o-ver all doth reign, who once on earth, the in-car-nate Word, for ran-somed sin-ners slain, now lives in realms of light, where saints with an-gels sing their songs be-fore him day and night, their God, Re-deem-er, King.

5. Crown him the Lord of heaven, en-throned in worlds a-bove; crown him the King, to whom is given, the won-drous name of Love. Crown him with man-y crowns, as thrones be-fore him fall, crown him, ye kings, with man-y crown, for he is King of all.

DAY BY DAY

words by
Carolina Sandell Bergh
trans. by Andrew L. Skoog

music by
Oscar Ahnfelt

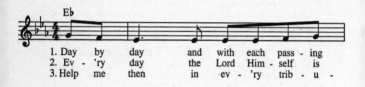

1. Day   by   day   and with each pass - ing
2. Ev - 'ry day   the Lord Him - self is
3. Help me then   in   ev - 'ry trib - u -

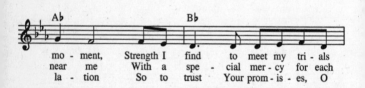

mo - ment, Strength I find   to meet my tri - als
near me   With a   spe - cial mer - cy for each
la - tion   So to trust Your prom - is - es, O

here;   Trust - ing in   my Fa - ther's wise be -
hour;   All my cares   He fain would bear, and
Lord,   That I lose   not faith's sweet con - so -

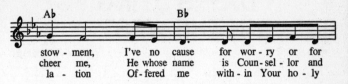

stow - ment, I've no cause for wor - ry or for
cheer me, He whose name is Coun - sel - lor and
la - tion Of - fered me with - in Your ho - ly

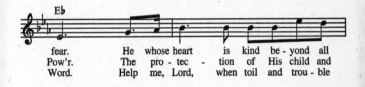

fear. He whose heart is kind be - yond all
Pow'r. The pro - tec - tion of His child and
Word. Help me, Lord, when toil and trou - ble

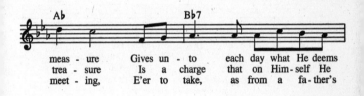

meas - ure Gives un - to each day what He deems
trea - sure Is a charge that on Him - self He
meet - ing, E'er to take, as from a fa - ther's

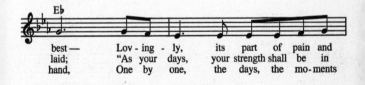

best — Lov - ing - ly, its part of pain and
laid; "As your days, your strength shall be in
hand, One by one, the days, the mo - ments

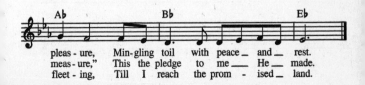

pleas - ure, Min - gling toil with peace __ and __ rest.
meas - ure," This the pledge to me __ He __ made.
fleet - ing, Till I reach the prom - ised __ land.

DAY IS DYING
IN THE WEST

words by
Mary A. Lathbury

music by
William F. Sherwin

1. Day is dy-ing in the west, Heav'n is touch-ing
2. Lord of life, be-neath the dome Of the u-ni-
3. While the deep-ening sha-dows fall, Heart of Love, en-
4. When for-ev-er from our sight Pass the stars, the

earth with rest; Wait and wor-ship while the night
verse, Thy home, Gath-er us, who seek Thy face,
fold-ing all, Thro' the glo-ry and the grace
day the night, Lord of an-gels on our eyes

Sets her eve-ning lamps a-light Thro' all the
To the fold of Thy em-brace, For Thou art
Of the stars that veil Thy face, Our hearts as-
Let e-ter-nal morn-ing rise, And sha-dows

Chorus

sky.
nigh.
cend.   Ho-ly, Ho-ly, Ho-ly
end!

Lord God of Hosts! Heav'n and earth are

full of Thee! Heav'n and earth are

prais-ing Thee, O Lord Most High!

DEAR LORD AND FATHER OF MANKIND

words by
John Greenleaf Whittier, 1872

music by
Frederick Charles Maker, 1887

1. *Dear Lord and Fa - ther of man - kind, For - give our fool - ish ways; Re - clothe us in our right - ful mind, In pur - er lives Thy ser - vice find, In deep - er rev - er - ence, praise.
2. In sim - ple trust like theirs who heard, Be - side the Syr - ian sea, The gra - cious call - ing of the Lord, Let us, like them, with - out a word Rise up and fol - low Thee.
3. O Sab - bath rest by Gal - i - lee, O calm of hills a - bove, Where Je - sus knelt to share with Thee The si - lence of e - ter - ni - y, In - ter - pret - ed by love!
4. Drop Thy still dews of qui - et - ness, Till all our striv - ings cease; Take from our souls the strain and stress, And let our or - dered lives con - fess The beau - ty of Thy peace.
5. Breathe through the heats of our de - sire, Thy cool - ness and Thy balm; Let sense be dumb, let flesh re - tire; Speak through the earth - quake, wind and fire, O still, small voice of calm!

*Or "Dear Lord, Creator good and kind."

ETERNAL FATHER, STRONG TO SAVE

words by
William Whiting (1825–1878), alt.

music by
Melita
John Bacchus Dykes (1823–1876)

1. E - ter - nal Fa - ther, strong to save, whose
2. O Christ, whose voice the wa - ters heard and
3. Most Ho - ly Spi - rit, who didst brood up -
4. O Trin - i - ty of love and power, thy

arm hath bound the rest - less wave, who
hushed their ra - ging at thy word, who
on the cha - os dark and rude, and
chil - dren shield in dan - ger's hour; from

bidd'st the might - y o - cean deep its
walk - edst on the foam - ing deep, and
bid its an - gry tu - mult cease, and
rock and tem - pest, fire and foe, pro -

own ap - point - ed lim - its keep: O hear us when we
calm a - mid its rage didst sleep: O hear us when we
give, for wild con - fu - sion, peace: O hear us when we
tect them where - so - e'er they go; thus ev - er - more shall

cry to thee for those in per - il on the sea.
cry to thee for those in per - il on the sea.
cry to thee for those in per - il on the sea.
rise to thee glad hymns of praise from land and sea.

FAIREST LORD JESUS

words by
C.E. Haupt

music by
C.E. Haupt

1. Fair - est Lord Je - sus, Ru - ler of all
2. Fair are the mea - dows, fair - er still the
3. Fair is the sun - shine, fair - er still the

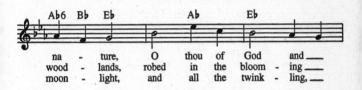

na - ture, O thou of God and ___
wood - lands, robed in the bloom - ing ___
moon - light, and all the twink - ling, ___

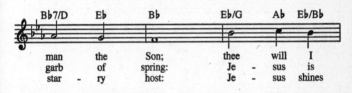

man the Son; thee will I
garb of spring: Je - sus is
star - ry host: Je - sus shines

cher - ish, thee will I hon - or, thou,
fair - er, Je - sus is pur - er, who
bright - er, Je - sus shines pur - er, than

my soul's glo - ry, joy, and crown.
makes the woe - ful heart to sing.
all the an - gels heaven can boast.

FAITH OF OUR FATHERS

words by
Frederick William Faber
(1814–1863), alt.

music by
St. Catherine,
Henri Frédéric Heny (1818–1888)
adapt. and arr. James G. Walton (1821–1905)

1. Faith of our fa - thers! liv - ing still
2. Faith of our fa - thers! faith and prayer
3. Faith of our fa - thers! we will love

in spite of dun - geon, fire and sword:
shall win all na - tions un - to thee;
both friend and foe in all our strife:

O how our hearts beat high with joy,
and through the truth that comes from God,
and preach thee, too, as love knows how,

when - e'er we hear that glo - rious word:
man - kind shall then in - deed be free.
by kind - ly deeds and vir - tuous life.

Refrain

faith of our fa - thers, ho - ly faith!

We will be true to thee till death.

FOR THE BEAUTY
OF THE EARTH

words by
Folliot S. Pierpoint, 1864

music by
Conrad Kocher, 1838
Arr. W.H. Monk, 1861

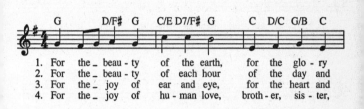

1. For the _ beau-ty of the earth, for the glo-ry
2. For the _ beau-ty of each hour of the day and
3. For the _ joy of ear and eye, for the heart and
4. For the _ joy of hu-man love, broth-er, sis-ter,

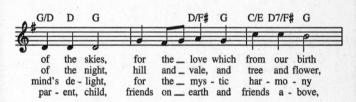

of the skies, for the _ love which from our birth
of the night, hill and _ vale, and tree and flower,
mind's de-light, for the _ mys-tic har-mo-ny
par-ent, child, friends on _ earth and friends a-bove,

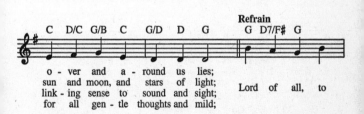

Refrain

o-ver and a-round us lies;
sun and moon, and stars of light;
link-ing sense to sound and sight;
for all gen-tle thoughts and mild;

Lord of all, to

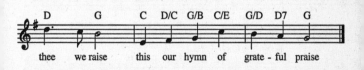

thee we raise this our hymn of grate-ful praise

FROM ALL THAT DWELL BELOW THE SKIES

words by
Isaac Watts, 1719

music by
Geistliche Kirchengesäng, 1623
Harm. Ralph Vaughan Williams, 1906

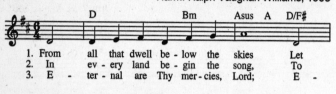

1. From all that dwell be-low the skies Let
2. In ev-ery land be-gin the song, To
3. E-ter-nal are Thy mer-cies, Lord; E -

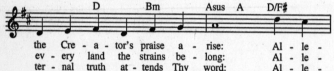

the Cre-a-tor's praise a-rise: Al-le-
ev-ery land the strains be-long: Al-le-
ter-nal truth at-tends Thy word: Al-le-

lu-ia! Al-le-lu-ia! Let the Re-deem-er's name be
lu-ia! Al-le-lu-ia! In cheer-ful sound all voic-es
lu-ia! Al-le-lu-ia! Thy praise shall sound from shore to

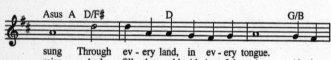

sung Through ev-ery land, in ev-ery tongue.
raise And fill the world with joy-ful praise. Al-le-
shore, Till suns shall rise and set no more.

lu-ia! Al-le-lu-ia! Al-le-lu-ia! Al-le-

lu-ia! Al-le-lu-ia!

GO TO DARK GETHSEMANE

words by
James Montgomery 1771–1854

music by
Richard Redhead 1820–1901

1. Go to dark Gethsemane,
2. Follow to the judgment hall,
3. Calv'ry's mournful mountain climb;
4. Early hasten to the tomb

All who feel the tempter's pow'r;
View the Lord of life arraigned;
There, adoring at his feet,
Where they laid his breathless clay;

Your Redeemer's conflict see.
Oh, the wormwood and the gall!
Mark that miracle of time.
All is solitude and gloom.

Watch with him one bitter hour;
Oh, the pangs his soul sustained!
God's own sacrifice complete.
Who has taken him away?

Turn not from his griefs away;
Shun not suff'ring, shame, or loss;
"It is finished!" hear him cry;
Christ is ris'n! He meets our eyes.

Learn from Jesus Christ to pray.
Learn from him to bear the cross.
Learn from Jesus Christ to die.
Savior, teach us so to rise.

GLORIOUS THINGS
OF THEE ARE SPOKEN

music by
Austria,

words by
John Newton (1725–1807), alt.

Franz Joseph Haydn (1732–1809)
desc. Michael E. Young (b. 1939)

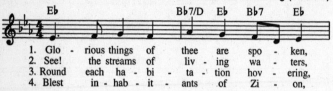

1. Glo - rious things of thee are spo - ken,
2. See! the streams of liv - ing wa - ters,
3. Round each ha - bi - ta - tion hov - ering,
4. Blest in - hab - it - ants of Zi - on,

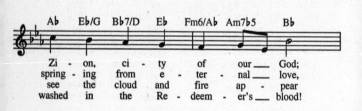

Zi - on, ci - ty of our ___ God;
spring - ing from e - ter - nal ___ love,
see the cloud and fire ap - pear
washed in the Re - deem - er's ___ blood!

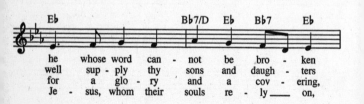

he whose word can - not be bro - ken
well sup - ply thy sons and daugh - ters
for a glo - ry and a cov - ering,
Je - sus, whom their souls re - ly ___ on,

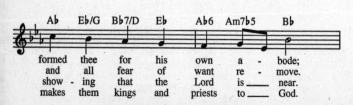

formed thee for his own a - bode;
and all fear of want re - move.
show - ing that the Lord is ___ near.
makes them kings and priests to ___ God.

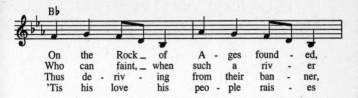

On the Rock of A - ges found - ed,
Who can faint, when such a riv - er
Thus de - riv - ing from their ban - ner,
'Tis his love his peo - ple rais - es

what can shake thy sure re - pose?
ev - er will their thirst as - suage?
light by night, and shade by day,
o - ver self to reign as kings:

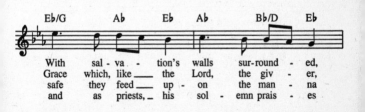

With sal - va - tion's walls sur - round - ed,
Grace which, like the Lord, the giv - er,
safe they feed up - on the man - na
and as priests, his sol - emn prais - es

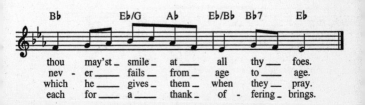

thou may'st smile at all thy foes.
nev - er fails from age to age.
which he gives them when they pray.
each for a thank of - fering brings.

GOD BE WITH YOU
TILL WE MEET AGAIN

words by
Jeremiah E. Rankin, 1880

music by
William G. Tomer, 1880

1. God be with you till we meet a - gain;
2. God be with you till we meet a - gain;
3. God be with you till we meet a - gain;
4. God be with you till we meet a - gain;

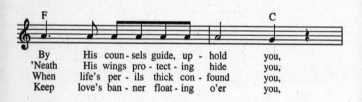

By His coun - sels guide, up - hold you,
'Neath His wings pro - tect - ing hide you,
When life's per - ils thick con - found you,
Keep love's ban - ner float - ing o'er you,

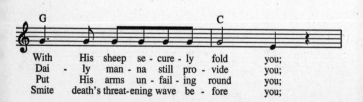

With His sheep se - cure - ly fold you;
Dai - ly man - na still pro - vide you;
Put His arms un - fail - ing round you;
Smite death's threat-ening wave be - fore you;

God be with you till we meet a - gain. Till we

meet, _____ till we meet, ___ Till we

meet at Je - sus' ___ feet, Till we

meet, _____ till we meet, ___ God be

with you till we meet a - gain.

GOD OF OUR FATHERS

words by
Daniel Crane Roberts (1841–1907)

music by
National Hymn,
George William Warren (1828–1902)

1. God of our fa - thers, whose al - might - y hand
   leads forth in beau - ty all the star - ry
   band of shin - ing worlds in
   splen - dor through the skies, our grate - ful
   songs be - fore thy throne a - rise.

2. Thy love di - vine hath led us in the past,
   in this free land by thee our lot is
   cast; be thou our ru - ler,
   guard - ian, guide, and stay, thy word our
   law, thy paths our cho - sen way.

3. From war's a - larms, from dead - ly pes - ti - lence,
   be thy strong arm our ev - er sure de -
   fense; thy true re - li - gion
   in our hearts in - crease, thy boun - teous
   good - ness nour - ish us in peace.

4. Re - fresh thy peo - ple on their toil - some way,
   lead us from night to nev - er - end - ing
   day; fill all our lives with
   love and grace di - vine, and glo - ry,
   laud, and praise be ev - er thine.

GOD WILL TAKE CARE OF YOU

words by
Civilla D. Martin, alt.

music by
W. Stillman Martin

1. Be not dis- mayed what- e'er be- tide,
2. Thru days of toil when your heart doth fail,
3. All you may need He will pro- vide,
4. No mat- ter what may be the test,

God will take care of you; Be- neath His wings of
God will take care of you; When dan- gers fierce your
God will take care of you; Noth- ing you ask will
God will take care of you; Lean, wea- ry one, up-

love a- bide, God will take care of you.
path as- sail, God will take care of you.
be de- nied, God will take care of you.
on His breast, God will take care of you.

God will take care of you, Thru ev- ery day,

o'er all the way; He will take care of you,

God will take care of you.

GUIDE ME O THOU GREAT JEHOVAH

words by
William Williams, 1745
Stanza 1 trans. Peter Williams, 1771
Stanzas 2–3 trans. William Williams, 1772

music by
John Hughes, 1907

1. Guide me, O Thou great Je-ho-vah, Pil-grim through this
2. O-pen now the crys-tal foun-tain, Whence the heal-ing
3. When I tread the verge of Jor-dan, Bid my anx-ious

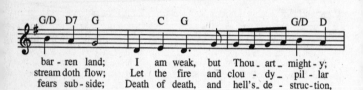

bar-ren land; I am weak, but Thou art might-y;
stream doth flow; Let the fire and clou-dy pil-lar
fears sub-side; Death of death, and hell's de-struc-tion,

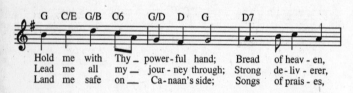

Hold me with Thy power-ful hand; Bread of heav-en,
Lead me all my jour-ney through; Strong de-liv-er-er,
Land me safe on Ca-naan's side; Songs of prais-es,

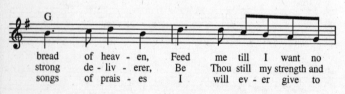

bread of heav-en, Feed me till I want no
strong de-liv-er-er, Be Thou still my strength and
songs of prais-es I will ev-er give to

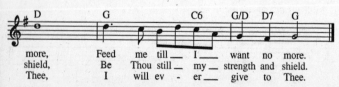

more, Feed me till I want no more.
shield, Be Thou still my strength and shield.
Thee, I will ev-er give to Thee.

HAVE THINE OWN
WAY LORD

words by
Adelaide Pollard, (w. 1902)

music by
George C. Stebbins, (w. 1907)

1. Have Thine own way, Lord! Have Thine own
2. Have Thine own way, Lord! Have Thine own
3. Have Thine own way, Lord! Have Thine own

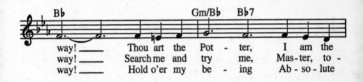

way! ___ Thou art the Pot - ter, I am the
way! ___ Search me and try me, Mas-ter, to -
way! ___ Hold o'er my be - ing Ab - so - lute

clay. ___ Mold me and make me Af - ter Thy
day! ___ Whit - er than snow, Lord, Wash me just
sway! ___ Fill with Thy Spir - it Till all shall

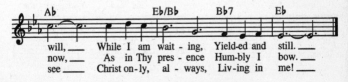

will, ___ While I am wait - ing, Yield-ed and still. ___
now, ___ As in Thy pres - ence Hum-bly I bow. ___
see ___ Christ on - ly, al - ways, Liv-ing in me! ___

HE AROSE

words by
Traditional Spiritual

music by
Traditional spiritual

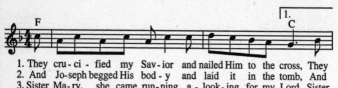

1. They cru - ci - fied my Sav - ior and nailed Him to the cross, They
2. And Jo-seph begged His bod - y and laid it in the tomb, And
3. Sister Ma-ry, she came run-ning, a - look-ing for my Lord, Sister
4. An an-gel came from heav-en and rolled the stone a - way, An

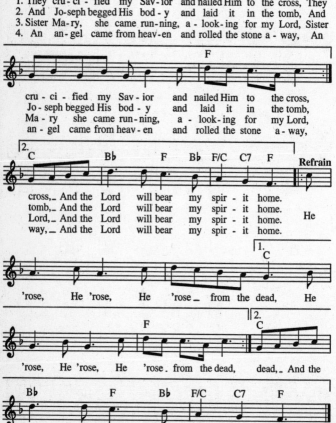

cru - ci - fied my Sav - ior and nailed Him to the cross,
Jo - seph begged His bod - y and laid it in the tomb,
Ma - ry she came run-ning, a - look-ing for my Lord,
an - gel came from heav - en and rolled the stone a - way,

cross, And the Lord will bear my spir - it home.
tomb, And the Lord will bear my spir - it home.
Lord, And the Lord will bear my spir - it home.
way, And the Lord will bear my spir - it home.

'rose, He 'rose, He 'rose from the dead, He

'rose, He 'rose, He 'rose from the dead, dead, And the

Lord shall bear my spir - it home.

HE HIDETH MY SOUL

words by
Fanny J. Crosby

music by
William J. Kirkpatrick

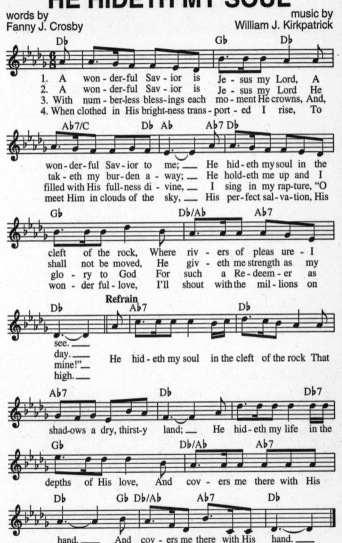

1. A won-der-ful Sav-ior is Je-sus my Lord, A won-der-ful Sav-ior to me; ___ He hid-eth my soul in the cleft of the rock, Where riv-ers of pleas-ure I see. ___
2. A won-der-ful Sav-ior is Je-sus my Lord He tak-eth my bur-den a-way; ___ He hold-eth me up and I shall not be moved, He giv-eth me strength as my day. ___
3. With num-ber-less bless-ings each mo-ment He crowns, And, filled with His full-ness di-vine, ___ I sing in my rap-ture, "O glo-ry to God For such a Re-deem-er as mine!" ___
4. When clothed in His bright-ness trans-port-ed I rise, To meet Him in clouds of the sky, ___ His per-fect sal-va-tion, His won-der-ful love, I'll shout with the mil-lions on high. ___

Refrain

He hid-eth my soul in the cleft of the rock That shad-ows a dry, thirst-y land; ___ He hid-eth my life in the depths of His love, And cov-ers me there with His hand, ___ And cov-ers me there with His hand. ___

HE LEADETH ME

words by
Joseph H. Gilmore, 1834–1918, alt.

music by
William B. Bradbury, 1816–1868

1. He lead - eth me: oh, bless - ed thought! Oh,
2. Some - times mid scenes of deep - est gloom, Some -
3. Lord, I would clasp thy hand in mine, Nor
4. And when my task on earth is done, When

words with heav'n - ly com - fort fraught! What -
times where E - den's bow - ers bloom, By
ev - er mur - mur nor re - pine; Con -
by thy grace the vic - t'ry's won, E'en

e'er I do, wher - e'er I be, Still 'tis God's hand that
wa - ters calm, o'er trou - bled sea, Still 'tis God's hand that
tent, what - ev - er lot I see, Since 'tis my God that
death's cold wave I will not flee, Since God through Jor - dan

lead - eth me.
lead - eth me. He lead - eth me, he
lead - eth me.
lead - eth me.

lead - eth me, By his own hand, he

lead - eth me. His faith - ful fol - l'wer

I would be, For by his hand he lead - eth me.

HE LIFTED ME

words by
Charles H. Gabriel

music by
Charles H. Gabriel

1. In loving kindness Jesus came, My soul in mercy to reclaim, And from the depths of sin and shame Thro' grace He lifted me.
2. He called me long before I heard, Before my sinful heart was stirred, But when I took Him at His word, Forgiv'n He lifted me.
3. His brow was pierced with many a thorn, His hands by cruel nails were torn, When from my guilt and grief, forlorn, In love He lifted me.
4. Now on a higher plane I dwell, And with my soul I know 'tis well; Yet how or why, I cannot tell, He should have lifted me.

Refrain

From sinking sand He lifted me, With tender hand He lifted me, From shades of night to plains of light, O praise His name, He lifted me!

HIS EYE IS ON THE SPARROW

words by
Civilla D. Martin, 1869–1948

music by
Charles H. Gabriel, 1856–1932

1. Why should I feel dis-cour-aged, _____ Why should the shad-ows come, _____ Why should my heart be lone-ly _____ And long for heaven and home, _____ When Je-sus is _____ my por-tion? _____ My con-stant friend _____ is He: _____ His

2. "Let not your heart be trou-bled," _____ His ten-der word I hear, _____ And rest-ing on His good-ness, _____ I lose my doubts and fears; _____ Though by the path _____ He lead-eth, _____ But one step I _____ may see: _____ His

3. When-ev-er I am tempt-ed, _____ When-ev-er clouds a-rise, _____ When songs give place to sigh-ing, _____ When hope with-in me dies, _____ I draw the clos-er to Him, _____ From care He sets _____ me free: _____ His

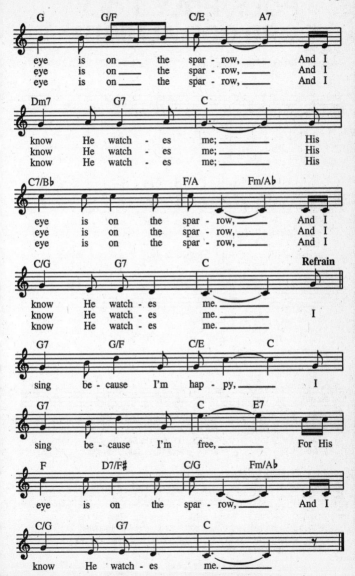

HOLY, HOLY, HOLY! LORD GOD ALMIGHTY

words by
Reginald Heber, 1783–1826, alt.

music by
John B. Dykes, 1823–1876

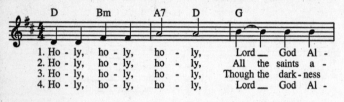

1. Ho - ly, ho - ly, ho - ly, Lord__ God Al -
2. Ho - ly, ho - ly, ho - ly, All the saints a -
3. Ho - ly, ho - ly, ho - ly, Though the dark - ness
4. Ho - ly, ho - ly, ho - ly, Lord__ God Al -

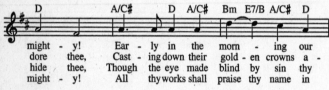

might - y! Ear - ly in the morn - ing our
dore thee, Cast - ing down their gold - en crowns a -
hide thee, Though the eye made blind by sin thy
might - y! All thy works shall praise thy name in

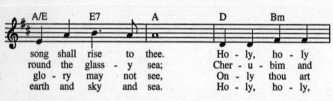

song shall rise to thee. Ho - ly, ho - ly
round the glass - y sea; Cher - u - bim and
glo - ry may not see, On - ly thou art
earth and sky and sea. Ho - ly, ho - ly,

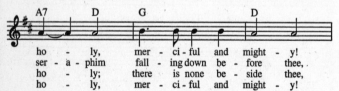

ho - ly, mer - ci - ful and might - y!
ser - a - phim fall - ing down be - fore thee,
ho - ly; there is none be - side thee,
ho - ly, mer - ci - ful and might - y!

God in three Per - sons, bless - ed Trin - i - ty!
Which wert and art and ev - er - more shalt be.
Per - fect in pow'r, in love and pu - ri - ty.
God in three Per - sons, bless - ed Trin - i - ty!

HOLY SPIRIT, TRUTH DIVINE

words by
Samuel Longfellow, 1864

music by
Adapt. from Orlando Gibbons, 1623

1. Ho - ly Spir - it, Truth di - vine,
2. Ho - ly Spir - it, Love di - vine,
3. Ho - ly Spir - it, Power di - vine,
4. Ho - ly Spir - it, Right di - vine,

dawn up - on this soul of mine;
glow with - in this heart of mine;
fill and nerve this will of mine;
King with - in my con - science reign;

Word of God and in - ward light,
kin - dle ev - ery high de - sire;
grant that I may strong - ly live,
be my Lord, and I shall be

wake my spir - it, clear my sight.
per - ish self in thy pure fire.
brave - ly bear, and no - bly strive.
firm - ly bound, for - ev - er free.

HOSANNA, LOUD HOSANNA

words by
Jennette Threlfall, 1873

music from
*Gesangbuch der herzogl, Wirtembergischen
Katholischen Hofkapelle, 1784*

1. Ho- san- na, loud ho- san- na, The lit- tle chil- dren sang; Through pil- lared court and tem- ple The love- ly an- them rang; To Je- sus, who had blessed them Close- fold- ed to his breast, The chil- dren sang their prais- es, The sim- plest and the best.

2. From Ol- i- vet they fol- lowed Mid an ex- ult- ant crowd, The vic- tor palm branch wav- ing, And chant- ing clear and loud; The Lord of men and an- gels Rode on in low- ly state, Nor scorned that lit- tle chil- dren Should on his bid- ding wait.

3. "Ho- san- na in the high- est!" That an- cient song we sing, For Christ is our Re- deem- er, The Lord of heaven our King. O may we ev- er praise him With heart and life and voice, And in his bliss- ful pres- ence E- ter- nal- ly re- joice.

HOW CAN A SINNER KNOW

words by
Charles Wesley, 1707-1788

music by
Lowell Mason, 1792-1872

1. How can a sin - ner know His sins on earth for - given? How can my gra - cious Sav - ior show My name in - scribed in heaven?
2. What we have felt and seen With con - fi - dence we tell; and pub - lish to the sons of men The signs in - fal - li - ble.
3. We who in Christ be - lieve That He for us hath died, We all His un - known peace re - ceive, And feel His blood ap - plied.
4. Ex - ults our ris - ing soul, Dis - bur - dened of her load, And swells un - ut - ter - a - bly full Of glo - ry and of God.
5. His love sur - pass - ing far The love of all be - neath, We find with - in our hearts, and dare The point - less darts of death.
6. Strong - er than death or hell The sa - cred power we prove; And, con - querors of the world, we dwell In heaven, who dwell in love.

HOW FIRM A FOUNDATION

words by
"K" in Rippon's *A Selection of Hymns*, 1787
(2 Tim. 2:19; Heb. 13:5; Is. 43:1–2)

music by
Early USA melody
harm. from Tabor, 1866

1. How firm a foun-da-tion, ye saints of the Lord, is laid for your faith in his ex-cel-lent word! What more can he say than to you he hath said, to you who for ref-uge to Je-sus have fled?

2. "Fear not, I am with thee, O be not dis-mayed, for I am thy God and will still give thee aid; I'll strength-en and help thee, and cause thee to stand up-held by my righ-teous, om-ni-po-tent hand.

3. "When through the deep wa-ters I call thee to go, the riv-ers of woe shall not thee o-ver-flow; for I will be with thee, thy trou-bles to bless, and sanc-ti-fy to thee thy deep-est dis-tress.

4. "The soul that on Je-sus still leans for re-pose, I will not, I will not de-sert to its foes; that soul, though all hell should en-deav-or to shake, I'll nev-er, no, nev-er, no, nev-er for-sake."

HOW I LOVE JESUS

words by
Frederick Whitfield

music by
Frederick Whitfield

1. There is a name I love to hear, I love to sing its worth; It sounds like music in mine ear, The sweetest name on earth.
2. It tells me of a Savior's love, Who died to set me free; It tells me of His precious blood, The sinner's perfect plea.
3. It tells me what my Father hath In store for ev'ry day; And, sunshine all the way.
4. It tells of One whose loving heart Can feel my deepest woe, Who none can bear below.

Chorus

O how I love Jesus! O how I love Jesus cause He first loved me.

O how I love Jesus! Be-

HOW SWEET THE NAME
OF JESUS SOUNDS

words by
John Newton

music by
Alexander R. Reinagle

1. How sweet the name of Je - sus sounds In
2. It makes the wound - ed spir - it whole And
3. Dear name! the rock on which I build, My
4. Je - sus, my Shep - herd, Broth - er, Friend, My
5. Till then I would Thy love pro - claim With

a be - liev - er's ear! It
calms the trou - bled breast; 'Tis
shield and hid - ing place; My
Proph - et, Priest and King, My
ev - 'ry fleet - ing breath; And

soothes his sor - rows, heals his wounds, And
man - na to the hun - gry soul And
nev - er - fail - ing treas - ure, filled With
Lord, my Life, my Way, my End, Ac -
may the mu - sic of Thy name Re -

drives a - way his fear.
to the wea - ry, rest.
bound - less stores of grace!
cept the praise I bring.
fresh my soul in death.

I AM THINE, O LORD

words by
Frances Jane Van Alstyne

music by
W.H. Doane

1. I am Thine, O Lord; I have heard Thy voice, And it
2. Con-se-crate me now to Thy ser-vice, Lord, By the
3. O the pure de-light of a sin-gle hour That be-
4. There are depths of love that I can-not know Till I

told Thy love to ____ me, But I
pow'r of grace di - vine; Let my
fore Thy throne I ____ spend, When I
cross the nar - row ____ sea; There are

long to rise in the arms of faith, And be
soul look up with a stead - fast hope, And my
kneel in prayer, and with Thee, my God, I com-
heights of joy that I may not reach Till I

clos - er drawn to Thee.
will be lost in Thine.
mune as friend with friend. Draw me near - er,
rest in peace with Thee.

Chorus

near - er, bless-ed Lord, To the cross where Thou hast

died, Draw me near - er, near - er,

near-er, bless-ed Lord, To Thy pre - cious bleed - ing side.

I HAVE DECIDED TO FOLLOW JESUS

words by
An Indian Prince

music by
Traditional
Arr. by Auila Read

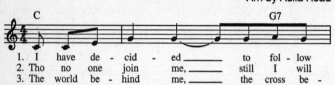

1. I have de-cid-ed ____ to fol-low
2. Tho no one join me, ____ still I will
3. The world be-hind me, ____ the cross be-

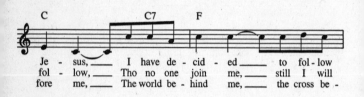

Je-sus, ____ I have de-cid-ed ____ to fol-low
fol-low, ____ Tho no one join me, ____ still I will
fore me, ____ The world be-hind me, ____ the cross be-

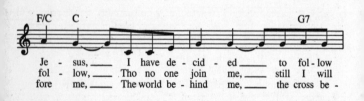

Je-sus, ____ I have de-cid-ed ____ to fol-low
fol-low, ____ Tho no one join me, ____ still I will
fore me, ____ The world be-hind me, ____ the cross be-

Je-sus, ____ No turn-ing back, ____ no turn-ing back! ____
fol-low, ____ No turn-ing back, ____ no turn-ing back! ____
fore me, ____ No turn-ing back, ____ no turn-ing back! ____

I LOVE THY KINGDOM, LORD

words by
Timothy Dwight

music by
Aaron Williams

1. I love Thy king - dom, Lord, The __
2. I love Thy Church, O __ God! Her __
3. For her my tears shall __ fall; For __
4. Be - yond my high - est __ joy I __
5. Sure as Thy truth shall __ last, To __

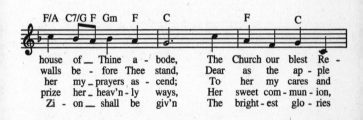

house of __ Thine a - bode, The Church our blest Re -
walls be - fore Thee stand, Dear as the ap - ple
her my prayers as - cend; To her my cares and
prize her __ heav'n - ly ways, Her sweet com - mun - ion,
Zi - on __ shall be giv'n The bright - est glo - ries

deem - er saved With His own __ pre - cious blood.
of Thine eye, And grav - en __ on Thy hand.
toils be giv'n, Till toils and __ cares shall end.
sol - emn vows, Her hymns of __ love and praise.
earth can yield, And bright - er __ bliss of heav'n.

I LOVE TO TELL
THE STORY

words by
A. Catherine Hankey

music by
William G. Fischer

1. I love to tell the sto — ry of un — seen things _ a — bove, Of Je — sus and His glo — ry, of _ Je — sus and _ His love; I love to tell the sto — ry be —
2. I love to tell the sto — ry 'tis pleas — ant to _ re — peat What seems, each time I tell it, more _ won — der — ful — ly sweet; I love to tell the sto — ry, for
3. I love to tell the sto — ry, for those who know _ it best Seem hun — ger — ing and thirst — ing to _ hear it like _ the rest; And love to tell the sto — ry when in scenes of glo — ry I

I MUST TELL JESUS

words and music by
E.A. Hoffman, 1894

1. I must tell Je - sus all of my
2. I must tell Je - sus all of my
3. O how the world to e - vil al -

tri - als; I can not bear these bur-dens a -
trou - bles; He is a kind, com - pas-sion-ate
lures me! O how my heart is tempt-ed to

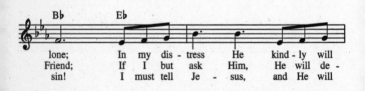

lone; In my dis - tress He kind - ly will
Friend; If I but ask Him, He will de -
sin! I must tell Je - sus, and He will

help me; He ev - er loves and cares for His own.
liv - er, Make of my trou - bles quick-ly an end.
help me O - ver the world the vic-t'ry to win.

89

Refrain

I must tell Jesus! I must tell

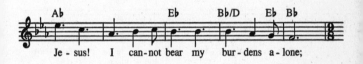

Je - sus! I can-not bear my bur-dens a - lone;

I must tell Je - sus! I must tell

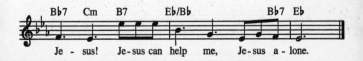

Je - sus! Je-sus can help me, Je-sus a - lone.

I NEED THEE EVERY HOUR

words by
Annie S. Hawks (w. 1872)

music by
Robert Lowry (w. 1872)

1. I need Thee ev-'ry hour, Most gra - cious Lord; No ten - der voice like Thine Can peace af - ford.
2. I need Thee ev-'ry hour: Stay Thou near by; Temp - ta - tions lose their pow'r When Thou art nigh.
3. I need Thee ev-'ry hour, In joy or pain; Come quick-ly and a bide, Or life is vain.
4. I need Thee ev-'ry hour, Most Ho - ly One; O make me Thine in dee, Thou bless - ed Son!

Refrain

I need Thee, O I need Thee; Ev - 'ry hour I need Thee! O bless me now, my Sav - ior: I come to Thee!

I SING THE MIGHTY POW'R OF GOD

words by
Isaac Watts, 1715

music by
*Gesangbuch der Herzogl, Wirtembergischen
Katholischen Hofkapelle, 1784 1868*

1. I sing the mighty power of God That made the mountains rise; That spread the flowing seas abroad And built the lofty skies. I sing the wisdom that ordained The sun to rule the day; The moon shines full at God's command, And all the stars obey.

2. I sing the goodness of the Lord That filled the earth with food; God formed the creatures with a word And then pronounced them good. Lord, how Thy wonders are displayed, Wher-e'er I turn my eyes; If I survey the ground I tread, Or gaze upon the skies!

3. There's not a plant or flower below But makes Thy glories known; And clouds arise, and tempests blow, By order from Thy throne; While all that borrows life from Thee Is ever in Thy care, And everywhere that we can be, Thou, God, art present there.

I SURRENDER ALL

words by
J.W. Van Deventer

music by
W.S. Weeden

1. All to Jesus I surrender; All to Him I freely give; I will ever love and trust Him, in His presence daily live.
2. All to Jesus I surrender; humbly at His feet I bow, worldly pleasures all forsaken; take me, Jesus, take me now.
3. All to Jesus I surrender; make me, Savior, wholly thine; let me feel the Holy Spirit, truly know that Thou art mine.
4. All to Jesus I surrender; Lord, I give my self to Thee; fill me with Thy love and power; let Thy blessing fall on me.
5. All to Jesus I surrender; now I feel the sacred flame. O the joy of full salvation! Glory, glory to His name!

Refrain

I surrender all, I surrender all, all to Thee, my blessed Savior, I surrender all.

I WILL SING THE WONDROUS STORY

words by
Francis H. Rowley

music by
Peter P. Bilhorn

1. I will sing the won-drous sto - ry Of the
2. I was lost but Je - sus found me, Found the
3. I was bruised but Je - sus healed me, Faint was
4. Days of dark - ness still come o'er me, Sor - row's

Christ who died for me; How He left His home in
sheep that went a - stray, Threw His lov - ing arms a -
I from man - y a fall; Sight was gone, and fears pos-
paths I oft - en tread; But the Sav - ior still is

glo - ry For the cross of Cal - va - ry.
round me, Drew me back in - to His way.
sessed me, But He freed me from them all.
with me, By His hand I'm safe - ly led.

Yes,_ I'll

sing _____ the won - drous sto - ry Of the

Christ _____ who died for me. Sing_ it with _____ the saints in

glo - ry Gath - ered by _____ the crys - tal sea.

I WOULD BE TRUE

words by
Howard A. Walter, 1883–1918

music by
Joseph Y. Peek, 1843–1911

1. I would be true, for there are those who
2. I would be friend of all, the foe, the

trust me; I would be pure, for
friend - less; I would be giv - ing,

there are those who care; I would be
and for - get the gift; I would be

strong, for there is much to
hum - ble, for I know my

suf - fer; I would be brave, for
weak - ness; I would look up, and

there is much to dare, I would be
laugh and love and lift, I would look

brave, for there is much to dare.
up, and laugh and love and lift.

I'VE FOUND A FRIEND

words by
James G. Small, 1817-1888

music by
Arthur Sullivan, 1842-1900

1. I've found a Friend, O such a Friend! He loved me ere I knew Him; He drew me with the cords of love, And thus He bound me to Him; And round my heart still close-ly twine Those ties which naught can sever, For I am His, and He is mine, For-ev-er and for-ev-er.

2. I've found a Friend, O such a Friend! He bled, He died to save me; And not a-lone the gift of life, But His own self He gave me. Naught that I have mine own I call, I'll hold it for the giv-er; My heart, my strength, my life, my all Are His, and His for-ev-er.

3. I've found a Friend, O such a Friend! So kind and true and ten-der, So wise a coun-sel-lor and guide, So might-y a de-fend-er! From Him who loves me now so well, What power my soul shall sev-er? Shall life or death, shall earth or hell? No! I am His for-ev-er.

IF YOU WILL ONLY
LET GOD GUIDE YOU

words and music by
Georg Neumark, 1657

1. If you will on - ly let God guide you, And hope in him through all your ways, What - ev - er comes, he'll stand be - side you,

2. On - ly be still, and wait his lei - sure In cheer - ful hope, with heart con - tent To take what - e'er the Fa - ther's plea - sure

3. Sing, pray, and swerve not from his ways, But do your part in con - science true; Trust his rich prom - is - es of grace,

97

IMMORTAL, INVISIBLE

words by
Walter Chalmers Smith,
1867 1987

music by
Adapted in *Caniadan y Cyssegr*, 1839

1. Im - mor - tal, in - vis - i - ble, God on - ly wise, In light in - ac - ces - si - ble hid from our eyes. Most bless - ed, most glo - rious, the An - cient of Days, Al - might - y, vic - to - rious, Thy great name we praise.
2. Un - rest - ing, un - hast - ing, and si - lent as light, Nor want - ing, nor wast - ing, Thou rul - est in might; Thy jus - tice like moun - tains high soar - ing a - bove Thy clouds, which are foun - tains of good - ness and love.
3. To all, life Thou giv - est, to both great and small; In all life Thou liv - est, the true life of all; We blos - som and flour - ish like leaves on the tree, Then with - er and per - ish; but naught chang - eth Thee.
4. Thou reign - est in glo - ry, Thou rul - est in light, Thine an - gels a - dore Thee, all veil - ing their sight; All praise we would ren - der; O help us to see 'Tis on - ly the splen - dor of light hid - eth Thee!

IN CHRIST THERE IS NO EAST OR WEST

words by
John Oxenham, 1908

music by
Alexander Robert Reinagle, 1836

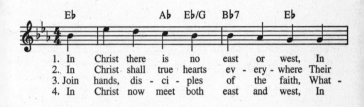

1. In   Christ there is   no   east   or   west,   In
2. In   Christ shall true hearts ev - ery - where Their
3. Join hands, dis - ci - ples of   the   faith, What -
4. In   Christ now meet both   east and   west,   In

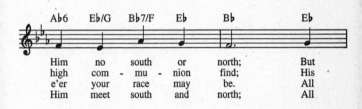

Him   no   south   or   north;   But
high   com - mu -   nion   find;   His
e'er   your race   may   be.   All
Him   meet south   and   north;   All

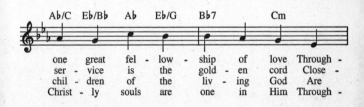

one   great fel - low - ship of   love Through -
ser - vice is   the   gold - en   cord Close -
chil - dren of   the   liv - ing God   Are
Christ - ly souls are   one   in   Him Through -

out   the   whole wide earth.
bind - ing hu -   man   kind.
sure - ly   kin   to   me.
out   the   whole wide earth.

IN CHRIST THERE IS
NO EAST OR WEST
(Second Tune)

words by
John Oxenham

African-American melody

1. In ___ Christ there is no ___ East or West, In
2. In ___ him shall true hearts ___ ev - ery - where Their
3. Join ___ hands, then, broth - ers ___ of the faith, What -
4. In ___ Christ now meet both ___ East and West, In

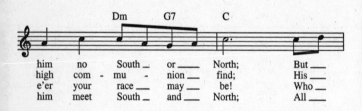

him no South ___ or ___ North; But ___
high com - mu - nion ___ find; His ___
e'er your race ___ may ___ be! Who ___
him meet South ___ and ___ North; All ___

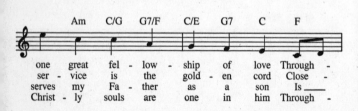

one great fel - low - ship of love Through -
ser - vice is the gold - en cord Close -
serves my Fa - ther as a son Is ___
Christ - ly souls are one in him Through -

out ___ the whole ___ wide earth.
bind - ing all ___ man - kind.
sure - ly kin to me.
out ___ the whole ___ wide earth.

IN THE CROSS OF
CHRIST I GLORY

words by
John Bowring, 1825

music by
Ithamar Conkey, 1849

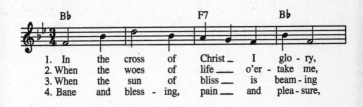

1. In the cross of Christ I glo-ry,
2. When the woes of life o'er-take me,
3. When the sun of bliss is beam-ing
4. Bane and bless-ing, pain and plea-sure,

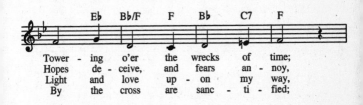

Tow-er - ing o'er the wrecks of time;
Hopes de - ceive, and fears an-noy,
Light and love up - on my way,
By the cross are sanc-ti - fied;

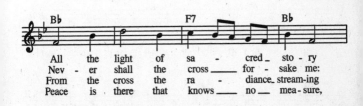

All the light of sa - cred sto - ry
Nev - er shall the cross for - sake me:
From the cross the ra - diance stream-ing
Peace is there that knows no mea-sure,

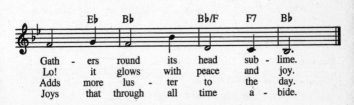

Gath - ers round its head sub - lime.
Lo! it glows with peace and joy.
Adds more lus - ter to the day.
Joys that through all time a - bide.

IN THE GARDEN

words by
C. Austin Miles

music by
C. Austin Miles

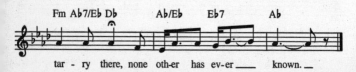

Ab

1. I come to the gar-den a - lone _____ while the
2. He speaks, and the sound of His voice _____ is so
3. I'd stay in the gar-den with Him _____ though the

Db

dew is still on the ros - es, And the
sweet the birds hush their sing - ing, And the
night a - round me be fall - ing, But He

Eb7   Ab   Bb7

voice I hear fall-ing on my ear, The Son of God dis-
mel - o - dy that He gave to me With - in my heart is
bids me go; thru the voice of woe His voice to me is

Eb   Eb7   Ab   Eb

clos - es.
ring - ing. And He walks with me, and He talks with me, and He
call - ing.

Eb7   Ab   C7

tells me I am His own; ____ and the joy we share as we

Fm   Ab7/Eb   Db   Ab/Eb   Eb7   Ab

tar - ry there, none oth-er has ev-er ____ known. ____

IN THE HOUR OF TRIAL

words by
James Montgomery, 1771–1854
Alt. Frances A. Hutton, 1811–1877

music by
Spencer Lane, 1843–1903

1. In the hour of tri - al,
Je - sus, plead for me;
Lest by base de -
ni - al, I de - part from Thee.
When Thou seest me wa - ver,
With a look re - call,
Nor for fear or
fa - vor Suf - fer me to fall.

2. With for - bid - den plea - sures
Would this vain world charm,
Or its sor - did
trea - sures Spread to work me harm;
Bring to my re - mem - brance
Sad Geth - sem - a - ne, _____
Or, in dark - er
sem - blance, Cross-crowned Cal - va - ry.

3. Should Thy mer - cy send me
Sor - row, toil, and woe,
Or should pain at -
tend me On my path be - low,
Grant that I may nev - er
Fail Thy hand to see: _____
Grant that I may
ev - er Cast my care on Thee.

4. When my last hour com - eth,
Fraught with strife and pain,
When my dust re -
turn - eth To the dust a - gain,
On Thy truth re - ly - ing,
Through that mor - tal strife: _____
Je - sus, take me,
dy - ing, To e - ter - nal life.

104
IN THE SWEET BY AND BY

words by
Sanford F. Bennet

music by
Joseph P. Webster

1. There's a land that is fair - er than day, And by
2. We shall sing on that beau - ti - ful shore The me -
3. To our boun - ti - ful Fa - ther a - bove We will

faith we can see it a - far, For the
lo - di - ous songs of the blest; And our
of - fer our trib - ute of praise, For the

Fa - ther waits o - ver the way To pre-pare us a dwell-ing place
spir - its shall sor - row no more Not a sigh for the bless - ing of
glo - ri - ous gift of His love And the bless-ings that hal - low our

Refrain

there. In the sweet by and by, We shall
rest.
days.

meet on that beau - ti - ful shore; In the sweet by and

by, We shall meet on that beau - ti - ful shore.

IS IT FOR ME?

words by
Frances R. Havergal, 1871

music by
Tullius C. O'Kane, 1871

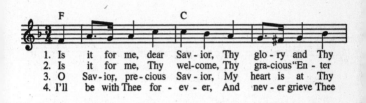

1. Is it for me, dear Sav-ior, Thy glo-ry and Thy
2. Is it for me, Thy wel-come, Thy gra-cious "En-ter
3. O Sav-ior, pre-cious Sav-ior, My heart is at Thy
4. I'll be with Thee for-ev-er, And nev-er grieve Thee

rest ___ For me, so weak and sin-ful! O
in" ___ For me Thy "Come ye bless-ed," For
feet; ___ I bless Thee, and I love Thee, And
more; ___ Dear Sav-ior, I must praise Thee, And

Refrain

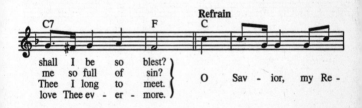

shall I be so blest?)
me so full of sin?
Thee I long to meet.
love Thee ev-er-more.

O Sav-ior, my Re-

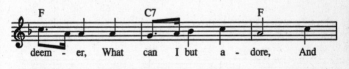

deem-er, What can I but a-dore, And

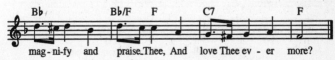

mag-ni-fy and praise Thee, And love Thee ev-er more?

IT IS WELL
WITH MY SOUL

words by
Horatio G. Spafford

music by
Phillip P. Bliss

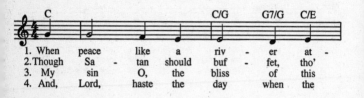

1. When   peace   like   a   riv - er   at -
2. Though   Sa -   tan   should   buf - fet,   tho'
3. My   sin   O,   the   bliss   of   this
4. And,   Lord,   haste   the   day   when   the

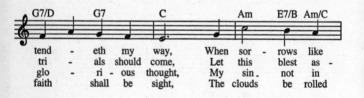

tend - eth   my   way,   When sor - rows like
tri - als should come, Let this blest as -
glo - ri - ous thought, My sin not in
faith shall be sight, The clouds be rolled

sea - bil - lows roll;   What - ev - er my
sur - ance con - trol, That Christ has re -
part but the whole, Is nailed to the
back as   a scroll, The trump shall re -

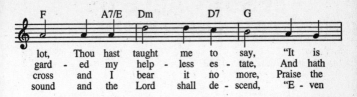

F	A7/E	Dm	D7	G

lot, Thou hast taught me to say, "It is
gard - ed my help - less es - tate, And hath
cross and I bear it no more, Praise the
sound and the Lord shall de - scend, "E - ven

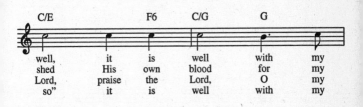

C/E		F6	C/G	G

well, it is well with my
shed His own blood with for my
Lord, praise the Lord, O my
so" it is well with my

C			G	

soul." It is well
soul. It is
soul!
soul.

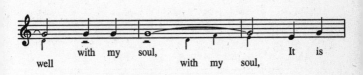

with my soul, with my soul, It is
well

F			C/G	G		C

well, it is well with my soul.

JESUS CALLS US O'ER THE TUMULT

words by
Cecil Frances Alexander, 1852
(Mt. 4:18–22)

music by
William H. Jude, 1874

1. Je - sus calls us o'er the tu - mult of our life's wild, rest - less sea; day by day his sweet voice sound - eth, say - ing, "Chris - tian, fol - low, me!"
2. As of old the a - pos - tles heard it by the Gal - i - le - an lake, turned from home and toil and kin - dred, leav - ing all for Je - sus' sake.
3. Je - sus calls us from the wor - ship of the vain world's gold - en store, from each i - dol that would keep us, say - ing, "Chris - tian, love me more!"
4. In our joys and in our sor - rows, days of toil and hours of ease, still he calls, in cares and plea - sures, "Chris - tian, love me more than these!"
5. Je - sus calls us! By thy mer - cies, Sav - ior, may we hear thy call, give our hearts to thine o - be - dience, serve and love thee best of all.

JESUS IS ALL THE WORLD TO ME

words by
Will L. Thompson

music by
Will L. Thompson

1. Je - sus is all the world to me, My life, my joy, my all; He is my strength from day to day, With - out Him I would fall. When I am sad to Him I go, No oth - er one can cheer me so; When I am sad He makes me glad, He's my Friend.

2. Je - sus is all the world to me, My Friend in tri - als sore; I go to Him for bless - ings, and He gives them o'er and o'er. He sends the sun - shine and the rain, He sends the har - vest's gold - en grain; Sun - shine and rain, har - vest of grain, He's my Friend.

3. Je - sus is all the world to me, And true to Him I'll be; O how could I this Friend de - ny, When He's so true to me? Fol - low - ing Him I know I'm right, He watch - es o'er me day and night; Fol - low - ing Him by day and night, He's my Friend.

4. Je - sus is all the world to me, I want no bet - ter friend; I trust Him now, I'll trust Him when Life's fleet - ing days shall end. Beau - ti - ful life with such a Friend; Beau - ti - ful life that has no end; E - ter - nal life, e - ter - nal joy, He's my Friend.

JESUS IS TENDERLY CALLING

words by
Fanny J. Crosby

music by
George C. Stebbins

1. Je - sus is ten - der - ly call - ing you home —
2. Je - sus is call - ing the wea - ry to rest —
3. Je - sus is wait - ing, O come to Him now —
4. Je - sus is plead - ing, O hear now His voice —

Call-ing to-day, call-ing to-day; Why from the sun-shine of
Call-ing to-day, call-ing to-day; Bring Him your bur-den and
Wait-ing to-day, wait-ing to-day; Come with your sins, at His
Hear Him to-day, hear Him to-day; They who be-lieve on His

love will you roam Far-ther and far-ther a - way? —
you shall be blest — He will not turn you a - way. —
feet low-ly bow — Come, and no long-er de - lay. —
name shall re-joice — Quick-ly a - rise and a - way. —

Call - ing to - day, Call - ing to -

day, Je - sus is call - ing, Is

ten - der - ly call - ing to - day. —

JESUS, LOVER OF MY SOUL

words by
Charles Wesley, 1740 (Wis. 11:26)

music by
Joseph Parry, 1879

1. Je - sus, lov - er of my soul, let me to thy
2. Oth - er ref - uge have I none, hangs my help - less
3. Thou, O Christ, art all I want, more than all in
4. Plen - teous grace with thee is found, grace to cov - er

bos - om fly, while the near - er wa - ters roll,
soul on thee; leave, ah! leave me not a - lone,
thee I find; raise the fall - en cheer the faint,
all my sin; let the heal - ing streams a - bound,

while the tem - pest still is high. Hide me, O my
still sup - port and com - fort me. All my trust on
heal the sick, and lead the blind. Just and ho - ly
make and keep me pure with - in. Thou of life the

Sav - ior, hide, till the storm of life is past;
thee is stayed, all my help from thee I bring;
is thy name, I am all un - righ - teous - ness;
foun - tain art, free - ly let me take of thee;

safe in - to the ha - ven guide;
cov - er my de - fense - less head
false and full of sin I am;
spring thou up with - in my heart;

O re - ceive my soul at last.
with the shad - ow of the wing.
thou art full of truth and grace.
rise to all e - ter - ni - ty.

JESUS, KEEP ME
NEAR THE CROSS

words by
Fanny J. Crosby

music by
William H. Doane

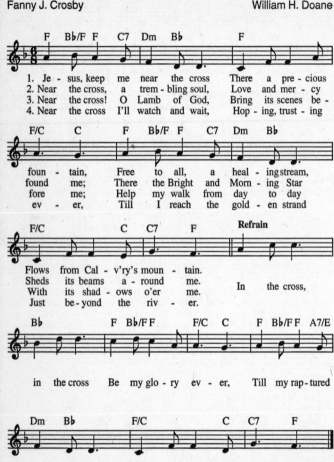

1. Je - sus, keep me near the cross There a pre - cious
2. Near the cross, a trem - bling soul, Love and mer - cy
3. Near the cross! O Lamb of God, Bring its scenes be -
4. Near the cross I'll watch and wait, Hop - ing, trust - ing

foun - tain, Free to all, a heal - ing stream,
found me; There the Bright and Morn - ing Star
fore me; Help my walk from day to day
ev - er, Till I reach the gold - en strand

Flows from Cal - v'ry's moun - tain.
Sheds its beams a - round me. In the cross,
With its shad - ows o'er me.
Just be - yond the riv - er.

in the cross Be my glo - ry ev - er, Till my rap - tured

soul shall find Rest, be - yond the riv - er.

JESUS, PRICELESS TREASURE

words by
Johann Franck
Tr. by Catherine Winkworth

music by
Adapted by Johann Cruger

1. Je-sus, price-less treas-ure, Source of pur-est
2. In Thy strength I rest me; Foes who would mo-
3. Ban-ished is our sad-ness! For the Lord of

pleas - ure, Tru - est Friend to me:
lest me Can - not reach me here.
glad - ness, Je - sus, en - ters in.

Long my heart hath pant-ed, 'Til it well-nigh
Tho the earth be shak-ing, Ev-ery heart be
Those who love the Fa - ther, Tho the storms may

faint-ed, Thirst-ing af-ter Thee. Thine I am, O
quak-ing, God dis-pels our fear. Sin and hell in
gath-er, Still have peace with-in. Yea, what-e'er we

spot-less Lamb, I will suf-fer nought to
con-flict fell With their heav-iest storms as -
here must bear, Still in Thee lies pur-est

hide Thee, Ask for naught be-side Thee.
sail us; Je-sus will not fail us.
pleas - ure, Je-sus, price-less treas - ure!

JESUS SAVES!

words by
Priscilla J. Owens

music by
William J. Kirkpatrick

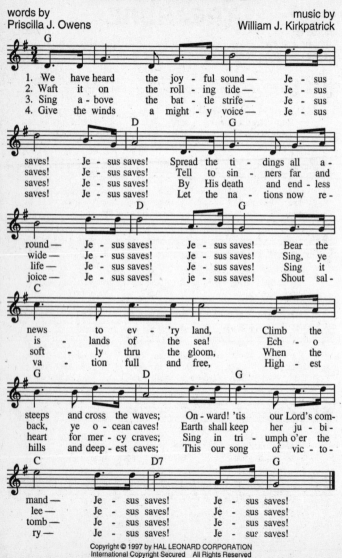

1. We have heard the joy-ful sound— Je-sus
2. Waft it on the roll-ing tide— Je-sus
3. Sing a-bove the bat-tle strife— Je-sus
4. Give the winds a might-y voice— Je-sus

saves! Je-sus saves! Spread the ti-dings all a-
saves! Je-sus saves! Tell to sin-ners far and
saves! Je-sus saves! By His death and end-less
saves! Je-sus saves! Let the na-tions now re-

round— Je-sus saves! Je-sus saves! Bear the
wide— Je-sus saves! Je-sus saves! Sing, ye
life— Je-sus saves! Je-sus saves! Sing it
joice— Je-sus saves! je-sus saves! Shout sal-

news to ev-'ry land, Climb the
is-lands of the sea! Ech-o
soft-ly thru the gloom, When the
va-tion full and free, High-est

steeps and cross the waves; On-ward! 'tis our Lord's com-
back, ye o-cean caves! Earth shall keep her ju-bi-
heart for mer-cy craves; Sing in tri-umph o'er the
hills and deep-est caves; This our song of vic-to-

mand— Je-sus saves! Je-sus saves!
lee— Je-sus saves! Je-sus saves!
tomb— Je-sus saves! Je-sus saves!
ry— Je-sus saves! Je-sus saves!

JESUS, SAVIOR, PILOT ME

words by
Edward Hopper, 1871
(Mt. 8:23–27; Mk. 4:35–41; Lk. 8:22–25)

music by
John E. Gould, 1871

1. Je - sus, Sav - ior, pi - lot me o - ver life's tem - pes - tuous sea; un - known waves be - fore me roll, hid - ing rock and treach - erous shoal. Chart and com - pass came from thee; Je - sus, Sav - ior, pi - lot me.

2. As a moth - er stills her child, thou canst hush the o - cean wild; bois - terous waves o - bey thy will, when thou sayest to them, "Be still!" Won - drous sov - ereign of the sea, Je - sus, Sav - ior, pi - lot me.

3. When at last I near the shore, and the fear - ful break - ers roar 'twixt me and the peace - ful rest, then, while lean - ing on thy breast, may I hear thee say to me, "Fear not, I will pi - lot thee."

JESUS SHALL REIGN

words by
Isaac Watts, 1674–1748, alt.

music by
attr. John Hatton, d. 1793

1. Je - sus shall reign wher - e'er the sun Does its suc - ces - sive jour - neys run; His king - dom stretch from shore to shore, Till moons shall wax and wane no more.
2. To him shall end - less prayer be made, And prais - es throng to crown his head; His name like sweet per - fume shall rise With ev - 'ry morn - ing sac - ri - fice.
3. Peo - ple and realms of ev - 'ry tongue Dwell on his love with sweet - est song; And in - fant voic - es shall pro - claim Their ear - ly bless - ings on his name.
4. Bless - ings a - bound wher - e'er he reigns: The pris - 'ners leap to lose their chains, The wea - ry find e - ter - nal rest, And all who suf - fer want are blest.
5. Let ev - 'ry crea - ture rise and bring Hon - ors pe - cu - liar to our King; An - gels de - scend with songs a - gain, And earth re - peat the loud a - men.

JESUS, THE VERY THOUGHT OF THEE

words by
Attr. Bernard of Clairvaux (1091–1153)
Trans. Edward Caswall, 1849 1987

music by
John Bacchus Dykes, 1866

1. Je - sus, the ver - y thought of
2. Nor voice can sing, nor heart can
3. O hope of ev - ery con - trite
4. But what to those who find? Ah,
5. Je - sus our on - ly joy be

Thee With sweet - ness fills my
frame, Nor can the mind re -
heart, O joy of all the
this Nor tongue nor pen can
Thou, As Thou our prize can wilt

breast; But sweet - er far Thy face to
call A sweet - er sound than Thy blest
meek, To those who fall, how kind Thou
show: The love of Je - sus, what it
be; Je - sus, be Thou our glo - ry

see, And in Thy pres - ence rest.
name, O Sav - ior of us all.
art! How good to those who seek!
is None but His loved ones know.
now, And through e - ter - ni - ty.

JESUS, THOU JOY OF LOVING HEARTS

words by
Attr. Bernard of Clairvaux (1091–1153)
Trans. Ray Palmer, 1858

music by
Henry Baker, 1854

1. Je - sus, Thou joy of lov - ing hearts, Thou fount of life, Thou light of all, From the best bliss that earth im - parts We turn, un - filled, ____ to heed Thy call.
2. Thy truth un - changed hath ev - er stood; Thou sav - est those that on Thee call; To them that seek Thee Thou art good, To them that find ____ Thee, all in all.
3. We taste Thee, O Thou liv - ing bread, And long to feast up - on Thee still; We drink of Thee, the foun - tain - head, And thirst our souls ____ from Thee to fill.
4. Our rest - less spir - its yearn for Thee, Wher - e'er our change - ful lot is cast, Glad when Thy gra - cious smile we see, Blest when our faith ____ can hold Thee fast.
5. O Je - sus ev - er with us stay, Make all our mo - ments calm and bright; O chase the night of sin a - way, Shed o'er the world ____ Thy ho - ly light.

JOYFUL, JOYFUL
WE ADORE THEE

words by
Henry van Dyke

music by
Ludwig van Beethoven; melody from
Ninth Symphony adapted by Edward Hodges

1. Joy - ful, joy - ful, we a - dore Thee,
2. All Thy works with joy sur - round Thee,
3. Thou art giv - ing and for - giv - ing,
4. Mor - tals, join the hap - py cho - rus

God of glo - ry, Lord of love; Hearts un - fold like
Earth and heaven re - flect Thy rays, Stars and an - gels
Ev - er bless - ing, ev - er blest, Well-spring of the
Which the morn - ing stars be - gan; Fa - ther love is

flowers be - fore Thee, Open - ing to the sun a - bove.
sing a - round Thee, Cen - ter of un - bro - ken praise.
joy of liv - ing, O - cean depth of hap - py rest!
reign - ing o'er us, Broth - er love binds man to man.

Melt the clouds of sin and __ sad - ness,
Field and for - est, vale and __ moun - tain,
Thou our Fath - er Christ, our __ Broth - er
Ev - er sing - ing, march we __ on - ward,

Drive the __ dark of doubt a - way; Giv - er of im -
Flow - ery __ mead - ow, flash - ing sea, Chant - ing bird and
All who __ live in love are Thine; Teach us how to
Vic - tors __ in the midst of strife, Joy - ful mu - sic

mor - tal glad - ness, Fill us with the light of day.
flow - ing foun - tain, Call us to re - joice in Thee.
love each oth - er, Lift us to the joy di - vine.
leads us sun - ward In the tri - umph song of life.

JUST AS I AM

words by
Charlotte Elliott

music by
William B. Bradbury

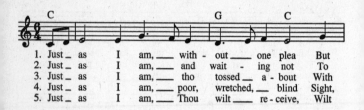

1. Just as I am, with-out one plea
2. Just as I am, and wait - ing not
3. Just as I am, tho tossed a-bout
4. Just as I am, poor, wretched, blind
5. Just as I am, Thou wilt re-ceive,

But
To
With
Sight,
Wilt

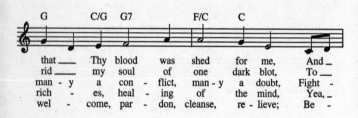

that Thy blood was shed for me, And
rid my soul of one dark blot, To
man - y a con - flict, man-y a doubt, Fight -
rich - es, heal - ing of the mind, Yea,
wel - come, par - don, cleanse, re - lieve; Be -

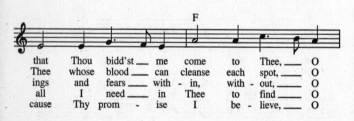

that Thou bidd'st me come to Thee, O
Thee whose blood can cleanse each spot, O
ings and fears with - in, with - out, O
all I need in Thee to find O
cause Thy prom - ise I be - lieve, O

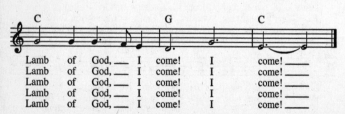

Lamb of God, I come! I come!
Lamb of God, I come! I come!
Lamb of God, I come! I come!
Lamb of God, I come! I come!
Lamb of God, I come! I come!

THE KING OF LOVE
MY SHEPHERD IS

words by
Henry Williams Baker (1821–1877);
para. of Psalm 23

music by
Dominus regit me,
John Bacchus Dykes (1823–1876)
desc. David Willcocks (b. 1919)

1. The   King   of   love   my   shep - herd   is,   whose
2. Where streams of   liv - ing   wa - ter   flow,   my
3. Per - verse and   fool - ish   oft   I   strayed,   but
4. In   death's dark vale   I   fear   no   ill   with
5. Thou spread'st a   ta - ble   in   my   sight;   thy
6. And   so   through all   the   length   of   days   thy

good - ness fail - eth   nev - er;   I
ran - somed soul   he   lead - eth,   and
yet   in   love   he   sought   me,   and
thee,   dear   Lord,   be - side   me;   thy
unc - tion grace   be - stow - eth;   and
good - ness fail - eth   nev - er: Good

noth - ing   lack   if   I   am   his   and
where   the   ver - dant   pas - tures   grow,   with
on   his   shoul - der   gent - ly   laid,   and
rod   and   staff   my   com - fort   still,   thy
oh,   what   trans - port   of   de - light   from
shep - herd   may   I   sing   thy   praise   with -

he   is   mine   for   ev - er.
food   ce - les - tial   feed - eth.
home,   re - joic - ing,   brought   me.
cross   be - fore   to   guide   me.
thy   pure   chal - ice   flow - eth!
in   thy   house   for   ev - er.

LEAD ON,
O KING ETERNAL

words by
Ernest W. Shurtleff

music by
Henry T. Smart

1. Lead on, O King E - ter - nal, The day of march has come; Hence - forth in fields of con - quest Your tents shall be our home. Through days of prep - a - ra - tion Your grace has made us strong, And now, O King E - ter - nal, We lift our bat - tle song.

2. Lead on, O King E - ter - nal, Till sin's fierce war shall cease, And ho - li - ness shall whis - per The sweet A - men of peace; For not with swords loud crash - ing, Nor roll of stir - ring drums, With deeds of love and mer - cy The heav'n - ly king - dom comes.

3. Lead on, O King E - ter - nal, We fol - low, not with fears; For glad - ness breaks like morn - ing Wher - e'er Your face ap - pears; Your cross is lift - ed o'er us; We jour - ney in its light; The crown a - waits the con - quest; Lead on, O God of might.

LEANING ON THE EVERLASTING ARMS

words by
Elisha A. Hoffman

music by
Anthony J. Showalter

1. What a fel - low-ship, what a joy di - vine,
2. O how sweet to walk in this pil - grim way,
3. What have I to dread, what have I to fear,

Lean - ing on the ev - er - last - ing arms;
Lean - ing on the ev - er - last - ing arms;
Lean - ing on the ev - er - last - ing arms?

What a bless - ed-ness, what a peace is mine,
O, how bright the path grows from day to day,
I have bless - ed peace with my Lord so near,

Lean - ing on the ev - er - last - ing arms.
Lean - ing on the ev - er - last - ing arms.
Lean - ing on the ev - er - last - ing arms.

Refrain

Lean - ing, lean - ing, Safe and se - cure from

all a - larms; Lean - ing, lean - ing,

Lean - ing on the ev - er - last - ing arms.

LET ALL MORTAL FLESH KEEP SILENCE

words from
the Liturgy of St. James

17th century French carol

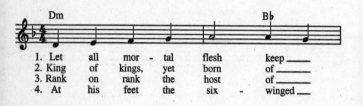

1. Let all mor - tal flesh keep ___
2. King of kings, yet born of ___
3. Rank on rank the host of ___
4. At his feet the six - winged ___

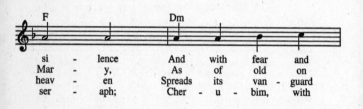

si - lence And with fear and
Mar - y, As of old on
heav - en Spreads its van - guard
ser - aph; Cher - u - bim, with

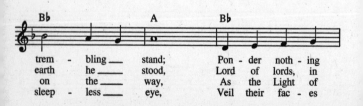

trem - bling ___ stand; Pon - der noth - ing
earth he ___ stood, Lord of lords, in
on the ___ way, As the Light of
sleep - less ___ eye, Veil their fac - es

125

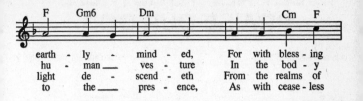

earth - ly - mind - ed, For with bless - ing
hu - man ___ ves - ture In the bod - y
light de - scend - eth From the realms of
to the ___ pres - ence, As with cease - less

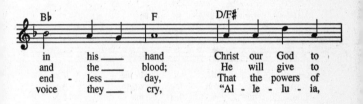

in his ___ hand Christ our God to
and the ___ blood; He will give to
end - less ___ day, That the powers of
voice they ___ cry, "Al - le - lu - ia,

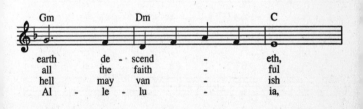

earth de - scend - eth,
all the faith - ful
hell may van - ish
Al - le - lu - ia,

Our full hom - age to de - mand.
His own self for heav - enly ___ food.
As the dark - ness clears a - way.
Al - le - lu - ia, Lord Most ___ High!"

LET ALL TOGETHER PRAISE OUR GOD

words by
Nikolaus Herman, 1560

music by
Nikolaus Herman, 1554

1. Let all to-geth-er praise our God Up-on his loft-y throne, For he un-clos-es heaven to-day And gives to us his Son, _____ And gives to us his Son.

2. He lays a-side his maj-es-ty And seems as noth-ing worth, And takes on him a serv-ant's form, Who made the heaven and earth, _____ Who made the heaven and earth.

3. Be-hold the won-der-ful ex-change Our Lord with us does make! Lo, he as-sumes our flesh and blood, And we of heaven par-take, _____ And we of heaven par-take.

4. The glo-rious gates of par-a-dise The an-gel guards no more; This day a-gain those gates un-fold. With praise our God a-dore, _____ With praise our God a-dore!

LET US BREAK
BREAD TOGETHER

words by
Traditional Negro Spiritual

music by
Traditional Negro Spiritual

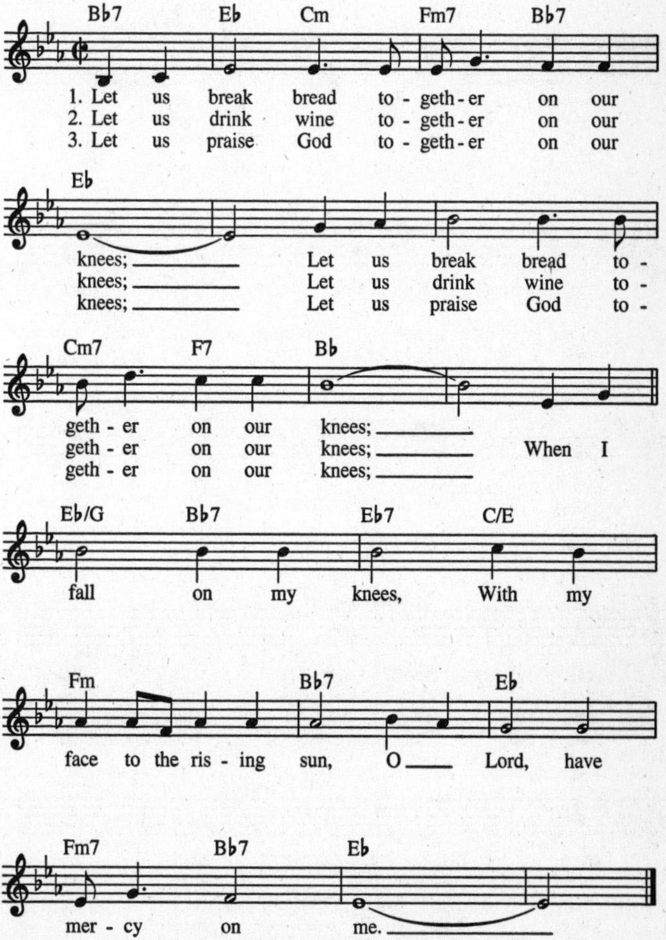

Bb7　　　Eb　　　Cm　　　Fm7　　　Bb7

1. Let us break bread to-geth-er on our
2. Let us drink wine to-geth-er on our
3. Let us praise God to-geth-er on our

Eb

knees; _____ Let us break bread to-
knees; _____ Let us drink wine to-
knees; _____ Let us praise God to-

Cm7　　　F7　　　Bb

geth-er on our knees; _____
geth-er on our knees; _____ When I
geth-er on our knees; _____

Eb/G　　　Bb7　　　Eb7　　　C/E

fall on my knees, With my

Fm　　　Bb7　　　Eb

face to the ris-ing sun, O ___ Lord, have

Fm7　　　Bb7　　　Eb

mer-cy on me. _____

LIFE IS LIKE A
MOUNTAIN RAILROAD

words by
M.E. Abbey

music by
Charles D. Tillman 1861–1943

1. Life is like a moun - tain rail - road, With an en - gi - neer that's brave; We must make the run suc - cess - ful From the cra - dle to the grave; Watch the curves, the fills, the
2. You will roll up grades of tri - al, You will cross the bridge of strife; See that Christ is your con - duct - or On this light - ning train of life; Al - ways mind - ful of ob -
3. You will of - ten find ob - struc - tions, Look for storms of wind and rain; On a fill or curve or tres - tle, They will al - most ditch your train; Put your trust a - lone in
4. As you roll a - cross the tres - tle, Span - ning Jor - dan's swell - ing tide; You be - hold the Un - ion De - pot In - to which your train will glide; There you'll meet the Su - p'rin

129

LET US WITH A GLADSOME MIND

words from
Psalm 136
paraphrased by John Milton, 1624

music by
John Antes, 1740-1811

1. Let us with a glad - some mind
2. Let us sound his name a - broad,
3. He, with all - com - mand - ing might,
4. All things liv - ing he does feed;
5. Let us then with glad - some mind

Praise the Lord, for he is kind:
For of gods he is the God:
Filled the new - made world with light:
His full hand sup - plies their need:
Praise the Lord, for he is kind:

For his mer - cies shall en - dure,

Ev - er faith - ful, ev - er sure.

LIFT HIGH THE CROSS

words by
George William Kitchin (1827–1912)
Rev. by
Michael Robert Newbolt, 1916

music by
Sidney Hugo Nicholson, 1916
Desc. Richard Proulx (b. 1937)

LIFT UP YOUR HEADS, O MIGHTY GATES

words by
Georg Weissel, 1642
Trans. by Catherine Winkworth, 1855

music by
Psalmodia Evangelica, 1789

1. Lift up your heads, O might-y gates; Be-hold, the King of glo-ry waits; The King of kings is draw-ing near; The Sav-ior of the world is here!
2. O blest the land, the cit-y blest, Where Christ the rul-er is con-fessed! O hap-py hearts and hap-py homes To whom this King in tri-umph comes!
3. Fling wide the por-tals of your heart; Make it a tem-ple set a-part From self-ish use for his em-ploy, A-dorned with prayer, and love, and joy.
4. Re-deem-er, come! We o-pen wide Our hearts to you; here, Lord, a-bide. Let us your in-ner pres-ence feel; Your grace and love in us re-veal.

LORD, FROM THE DEPTHS TO YOU I CRY

words from
Psalm 130, paraphrased in the
Scottish Psalter, 1650

music from
Prys's *Welsh Psalter*, 1621

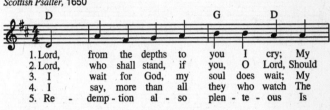

1. Lord, from the depths to you I cry; My
2. Lord, who shall stand, if you, O Lord, Should
3. I wait for God, my soul does wait; My
4. I say, more than all they who watch The
5. Re - demp - tion al - so plen - te - ous Is

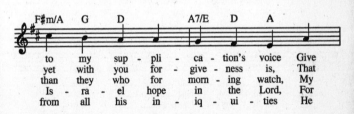

call, Lord, you will hear: Un-
mark in - iq - ui - ty? But
hope is in his word. More
morn - ing light to see. Let
ev - er found with him: And

to my sup - pli - ca - tion's voice Give
yet with you for - give - ness is, That
than they who for morn - ing watch, My
Is - ra - el hope in the Lord, For
from all his in - iq - ui - ties He

an at - ten - tive ear.
feared you still may be.
soul waits for the Lord.
with him mer - cies be.
Is - rael shall re - deem.

LORD, I WANT TO
BE A CHRISTIAN

words by
Traditional Negro Spiritual

music by
Traditional Negro Spiritual

1. Lord, I want to be a Chris-tian in my heart, in my heart;__ Lord, I want to be a Christian in my heart, in my heart. In my heart,_____ in my heart,_____ Lord, I want to be a Chrs-tian in my heart.
2. Lord, I want to be more lov-ing in my heart, in my heart;__ Lord, I want to be more lov-ing in my heart, in my heart. In my heart,_____ in my heart,_____ Lord, I want to be more lov-ing in my heart.
3. Lord, I want to be more ho-ly in my heart, in my heart;__ Lord, I want to be more ho-ly in my heart, in my heart. In my heart,_____ in my heart,_____ Lord, I want to be more ho-ly in my heart.
4. Lord, I want to be like Je-sus in my heart, in my heart;__ Lord, I want to be like Je-sus in my heart, in my heart. In my heart,_____ in my heart,_____ Lord, I want to be like Je-sus in my heart.

LORD SPEAK TO ME

words by
Frances Ridley Havergal, 1872   Adapt. from Robert Schumann, 1839
(Rom. 14:7)

music by

1. Lord, speak to me, that __ I may __ speak in
2. O strength-en me, that __ while I __ stand firm
3. O teach me, Lord, that __ I may __ teach the
4. O fill me with thy __ ful - ness, __ Lord, un-
5. O use me, Lord, use ev - en __ me, just

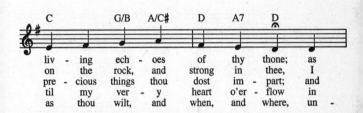

liv - ing ech - oes of thy thone; as
on the rock, and strong in thee, I
pre - cious things thou dost im - part; and
til my ver - y heart o'er - flow in
as thou wilt, and when, and where, un-

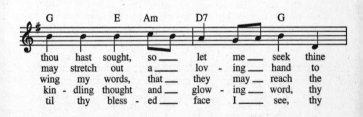

thou hast sought, so __ let me __ seek thine
may stretch out a __ lov - ing __ hand to
wing my words, that __ they may __ reach the
kin - dling thought and __ glow - ing __ word, thy
til thy bless - ed __ face I __ see, thy

err - ing chil - dren __ lost and lone.
wres - tlers with the __ trou - bled sea.
hid - den depths of __ many a heart.
love to tell, thy __ praise to show.
rest, thy joy, thy __ glo - ry share.

THE LORD'S
MY SHEPHERD

music by
Based on Psalm 23
Scottish Psaltyer

music by
Traditional
Arr. by John and Aquila Read

1. The Lord's my Shep-herd, I'll not want, He makes me down to lie In pas-tures green, He lead-eth me The qui-et wa-ters by; He lead-eth me, He lead-eth me, The qui-et wa-ters by.

2. My soul He doth re-store a-gain, And me to walk doth make With-in the paths of bless-ed-ness, E'en for His own name's sake; With-in the paths of bless-ed-ness E'en for His own name's sake.

3. Yea, tho I walk thru shad-owed vale, Yet will I fear no ill, For Thou art with me and Thy rod And staff me com-fort still; Thy rod and staff me com-fort still, com-fort still.

4. My ta-ble Thou hast fur-nish-ed In pres-ence of my foes. My head with oil Thou dost an-noint, And my cup o-ver-flows; My head with oil Thou dost an-noint, And my cup o-ver-flows.

5. Good-ness and mer-cy all my days Shall sure-ly fol-low me, And in my Fa-ther's house al-ways My dwell-ing place shall be; And in my heart for-ev-er-more Thy dwell-ing place shall be.

MINE EYES HAVE SEEN THE GLORY

words by
Julia Ward Howe

music by
William Steffe

1. Mine eyes have seen the glo - ry of the
2. I have seen Him in the watch - fires of a
3. He has sound - ed forth the trum - pet that shall

com-ing of the Lord; He is tram-pling out the vin-tage where the
hun-dred cir-cling camps, They have build - ed Him an al - tar in the
nev - er call re - treat, He is sift - ing out the hearts of men be-

grapes of wrath are stored; He hath loosed the fate - ful light-ning of His
eve-ning dews and damps; I can read His right-eous sen-tence by the
fore His judg-ment seat, Oh, be swift, my soul, to an - swer Him, be

ter - ri - ble swift sword; His truth is march - ing
dim and flar - ing lamps, His day is march - ing
ju - bi-lant, my feet, Our God is march - ing

Refrain

on.
on.
on.   Glo - ry, glo - ry hal - le - lu - jah!

Glo - ry, glo - ry hal - le - lu - jah!   Glo - ry, glo - ry hal - le -

ju - jah! His truth is march - ing on.

LOVE DIVINE,
ALL LOVES EXCELLING

words by
Charles Wesley

music by
John Zundel

1. Love di - vine, all loves ex - cel - ling,
2. Breathe, O breathe Thy lov - ing Spir - it
3. Come, al - might - y to de - liv - er,
4. Fin - ish then Thy new cre - a - tion,

Joy of heav'n to earth come down; Fix in us Thy
In - to ev - 'ry trou - bled breast! Let us all in
Let us all Thy life re - ceive; Sud - den - ly re -
Pure and spot - less let us be; Let us see Thy

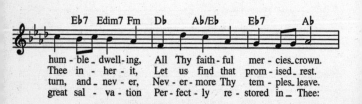

hum - ble dwell - ing, All Thy faith - ful mer - cies crown.
Thee in - her - it, Let us find that prom - ised rest.
turn, and nev - er, Nev - er - more Thy tem - ples leave.
great sal - va - tion Per - fect - ly re - stored in Thee:

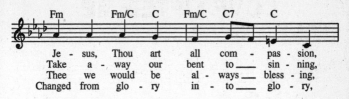

Je - sus, Thou art all com - pas - sion,
Take a - way our bent to sin - ning,
Thee we would be al - ways bless - ing,
Changed from glo - ry in - to glo - ry,

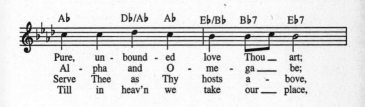

Pure, un - bound - ed love Thou art;
Al - pha and O - me - ga be;
Serve Thee as Thy hosts a - bove,
Till in heav'n we take our place,

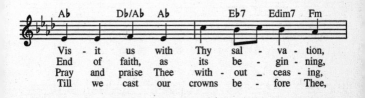

Vis - it us with Thy sal - va - tion,
End of faith, as its be - gin - ning,
Pray and praise Thee with - out ceas - ing,
Till we cast our crowns be - fore Thee,

En - ter ev - 'ry trem - bling heart.
Set our hearts at lib - er - ty.
Glo - ry in Thy per - fect love.
Lost in won - der, love and praise!

LOVE LIFTED ME

words by
James Rowe

music by
Howard E. Smith

1. I was sink - ing deep in sin,
2. All my heart to Him I give,
3. Souls in dan - ger, look a - bove,

Far from the peace - ful shore,_____
Ev - er to Him I'll cling,_____
Je - sus com - plete - ly saves;_____

Ver - y deep - ly stained with - in,
In His bless - ed pres - ence live,
He will lift you by His love

Sink - ing to rise no more;_____
Ev - er His prais - es sing;_____
Out of the an - gry waves;_____

But the Mas - ter of the sea
Love so might - y and so true
He's the Mas - ter of the sea,

Heard my de - spair - ing cry,_____
Mer - its my soul's best songs;_____
Bil - lows His will o - bey;_____

141

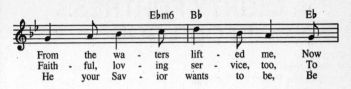

From the wa - ters lift - ed me, Now
Faith - ful, lov - ing ser - vice, too, To
He your Sav - ior wants to be, Be

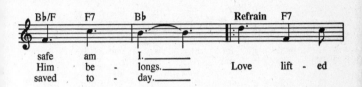

safe am I._____ Love lift - ed
Him be - longs._____
saved to - day._____

me!_____ Love lift - ed

me!_____ When noth - ing

else could help, Love lift - ed

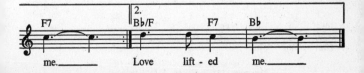

me._____ Love lift - ed me._____

A MIGHTY FORTRESS
IS OUR GOD

words by
Martin Luther
translated by Frederick H. Hedge;
based on Psalm 46

music by
Martin Luther

C		G Em Am D7 G	Am
1. A	might - y	for - tress is our God,	A
2. Did	we in	our own strength con - fide,	Our
3. And	tho this	world, with dev - ils filled,	Should
4. That	word a -	bove all earth - ly pow'rs,	No

Em F C Am Dm	G7	C	
bul - wark nev - er fail -	ing;		Our
striv - ing would be los -	ing,		Were
threat - en to un - do	us,		We
thanks to them, a - bid -	eth;		The

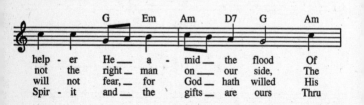

G Em Am D7 G	Am
help - er He a - mid the flood	Of
not the right man on our side,	The
will not fear, for God hath willed	His
Spir - it and the gifts are ours	Thru

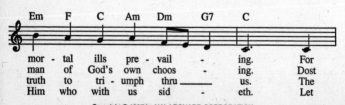

Em F C Am Dm	G7	C	
mor - tal ills pre - vail -	ing.		For
man of God's own choos -	ing.		Dost
truth to tri - umph thru	us.		The
Him who with us sid -	eth.		Let

143

MORE LOVE TO THEE

words by
Elizabeth P. Prentiss

music by
William H. Doane

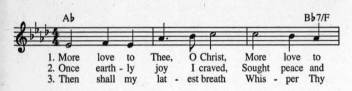

1. More love to Thee, O Christ, More love to
2. Once earth-ly joy I craved, Sought peace and
3. Then shall my lat-est breath Whis-per Thy

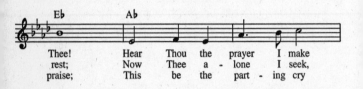

Thee! Hear Thou the prayer I make
rest; Now Thee a-lone I seek,
praise; This be the part-ing cry

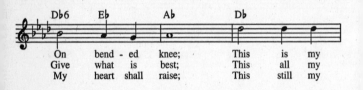

On bend-ed knee; This is my
Give what is best; This all my
My heart shall raise; This still my

ear-nest plea: More love, O Christ to Thee,
prayer shall be:
prayer shall be:

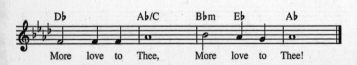

More love to Thee, More love to Thee!

MUST JESUS BEAR
THE CROSS ALONE

words by
Timothy Rees, 1946

music by
Welsh hymn melody;
harm. by David Evans, 1927

MY FAITH HAS FOUND
A RESTING PLACE

words by
Lidie H. Edmunds

music by
André Grétry
arranged by William J. Kirkpatrick

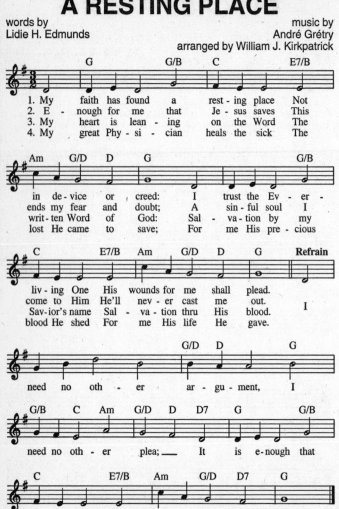

1. My faith has found a rest-ing place Not
2. E-nough for me that Je-sus saves This
3. My heart is lean-ing on the Word The
4. My great Phy-si-cian heals the sick The

in de-vice or creed: I trust the Ev-er-
ends my fear and doubt; A sin-ful soul I
writ-ten Word of God: Sal-va-tion by my
lost He came to save; For me His pre-cious

Refrain

liv-ing One His wounds for me shall plead.
come to Him He'll nev-er cast me out.
Sav-ior's name Sal-va-tion thru His blood.
blood He shed For me His life He gave.

I

need no oth-er ar-gu-ment, I

need no oth-er plea; ___ It is e-nough that

Je-sus died, And that He died for me.

MY FAITH LOOKS UP TO THEE

words by
Ray Palmer

music by
Lowell Mason

1. My faith looks up to Thee, Thou Lamb of
2. May Thy rich grace im-part Strength to my
3. While life's dark maze I tread And griefs a-
4. When ends life's pass-ing dream, When death's cold,

Cal - va - ry, Sav - ior di - vine!
faint - ing heart, My zeal in - spire;
round me spread, Be Thou my guide;
threat - ening stream Shall o'er me roll,

Now hear me while I pray, Take all my
As Thou hast died for me, O may my
Bid dark - ness turn to day, Wipe sor - row's
Blest Sav - ior, then, in love, Fear and dis -

guilt a - way, O let me
love to Thee Pure, warm, and
tears a - way, Nor let me
trust re - move; O lift me

from this day Be whol - ly Thine!
change - less be, A liv - ing fire!
ev - er stray From Thee a - side.
safe a - bove, A ran - somed soul!

MY HOPE IS BUILT
ON NOTHING LESS

words by
Edward Mote, 1834

music by
William B. Bradbury, 1863

1. My hope is built on noth-ing less than
2. When dark-ness veils his love-ly face, I
3. His oath, his cov-e-nant, his blood sup-
4. When he shall come with trum-pet sound, O

Je-sus' blood and righ-teous-ness. I
rest on his un-chang-ing grace. In
port me in the whelm-ing flood. When
may I then in him be found! Dressed

dare not trust the sweet-est frame, but
ev-ery high and storm-y gale, my
all a-round my soul gives way, he
in his righ-teous-ness a-lone, fault-

wholly lean on Je-sus' name. On
an-chor holds with-in the veil.
then is all my hope and stay.
less to stand be-fore the throne!

Refrain

Christ the sol-id rock I stand, all oth-er ground is

sink-ing sand; all oth-er ground is sink-ing sand.

NEARER MY GOD
TO THEE

words by
Sarah F. Adams;
based on Genesis 28:10–22

music by
Lowell Mason

1. Near - er, my God, to Thee, Near - er to Thee! E'en though it be a cross That rais - eth me; Still all my song shall be, Near - er, my God, to Thee, Near - er, my God, to Thee, Near - er to Thee.

2. Though like the wan - der - er, The sun gone down, Dark - ness be o - ver me, My rest a stone; Yet in my dreams I'd be Near - er, my

3. Then, with my wak - ing thoughts Bright with Thy praise, Out of my ston - y griefs, Beth - el I'll raise; So by my woes to be Near - er, my

4. Or if on joy - ful wing, Cleav - ing the sky, Sun, moon, and stars for - got, Up - ward I fly, Still all my song shall be, Near - er, my

NOW THANK WE ALL OUR GOD

words by
Martin Rinkart
translated by Catherine Winkworth

music by
Johann Crüger
harmonized by
Felix Mendelssohn

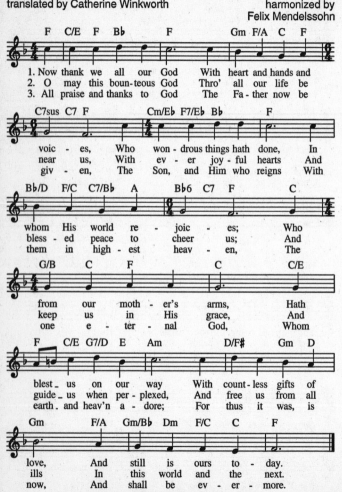

1. Now thank we all our God With heart and hands and voic-es, Who won-drous things hath done, In whom His world re-joic-es; Who from our moth-er's arms, Hath blest us on our way With count-less gifts of love, And still is ours to-day.

2. O may this boun-teous God Thro' all our life be near us, With ev-er joy-ful hearts And bless-ed peace to cheer us; And keep us in His grace, And guide us when per-plexed, And free us from all ills In this world and the next.

3. All praise and thanks to God The Fa-ther now be giv-en, The Son, and Him who reigns With them in high-est heav-en, The one e-ter-nal God, Whom earth and heav'n a-dore; For thus it was, is now, And shall be ev-er-more.

NOW THE DAY IS OVER

words by
Sabine Baring-Gould, 1865

music by
Joseph Barnby, 1868

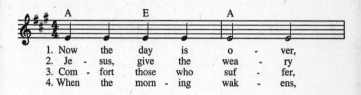

1. Now the day is o - ver,
2. Je - sus, give the wea - ry
3. Com - fort those who suf - fer,
4. When the morn - ing wak - ens,

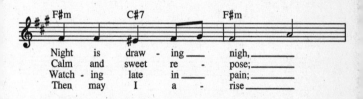

Night is draw - ing nigh,
Calm and sweet re - pose;
Watch - ing late in pain;
Then may I a - rise

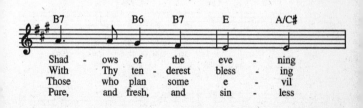

Shad - ows of the eve - ning
With Thy ten - derest bless - ing
Those who plan some e - vil
Pure, and fresh, and sin - less

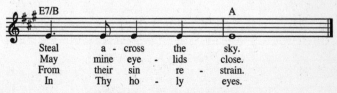

Steal a - cross the sky.
May mine eye - lids close.
From their sin re - strain.
In Thy ho - ly eyes.

O BROTHER MAN, FOLD TO YOUR HEART

words by
John Greenleaf Whittier, 1848, 1972

music by
Alfred Scott-Gatty, 1900

As in *The English Hymnal*, 1906

1. O broth - er man, fold to your heart your broth - er; Where pit - y dwells, the peace of God is __ there; __ To wor - ship right - ly is to love each oth - er, Each smile a hymn, each kind - ly deed a prayer.

2. For he whom Je - sus loved has tru - ly spo - ken: The hol - lier wor - ship which he deigns to __ bless __ Re - stores the lost, __ and binds the spir - it bro - ken, And feeds the wid - ow and the fa - ther - less.

3. Fol - low with rev - erent steps the great ex - am - ple Of him whose ho - ly work was do - ing __ good; __ So shall the wide __ earth seem our Fa - ther's tem - ple, Each lov - ing life a psalm of grat - i - tude.

4. Then shall all shack - les fall; the storm - y clang - or Of wild war mu - sic o'er the earth shall __ cease; __ Love shall tread out __ the bale - ful fire of an - ger, And in its ash - es plant the tree of peace.

O COME AND MOURN WITH ME AWHILE

words by
Frederick W. Faber, 1814–1863

music by
John Bacchus Dykes, 1823–1876

1. O come and mourn with me a-
2. Have we no tears to shed for
3. Seven times He spake seven words of
4. O love of God! O sin of

while; O come ye to the
Him, While sol-diers scoff and
love; And all three hours His
man! In this dread act your

Sav-ior's side; O come, to-
foes de-ride? Ah! look how
si-lence cried For mer-cy
strength is tried; And vic-to-

geth-er let us mourn:
pa-tient-ly He hangs:
on the souls of men:
ry re-mains with love:

Je-sus, our Lord, is cru-ci-fied!
Je-sus, our Lord, is cru-ci-fied!
Je-sus, our Lord, is cru-ci-fied!
Je-sus, our Lord, is cru-ci-fied!

O FOR A THOUSAND
TONGUES TO SING

words by
Charles Wesley, 1739

music by
Carl G. Gläser;
arr. by Lowell Mason, 1839

1. O   for   a   thou - sand   tongues to   sing   my
2. My   gra - cious Mas - ter   and   my God,   as -
3. Je - sus! the name   that   charms our fears,   that
4. He   breaks the power of   can - celed sin,   he
5. He   speaks, and listen - ing   to his voice,   new
6. Hear him, ye deaf;   his   praise, ye dumb,   your

great   Re - deem - er's   praise,   the
sist   me   to   pro -   claim,   to
bids   our sor - rows   cease;   'tis
sets   the pris - oner   free;   his
life   the dead   re -   ceive;   the
loos - ened tongues em -   ploy;   ye

glo - ries   of   my   God and King,   the ____
spread through all   the   earth a - broad the ____
mu - sic   in   the   sin - ner's ears, 'tis ____
blood can   make   the   foul - est clean; his ____
mourn - ful, bro - ken   hearts re - joice, the ____
blind, be - hold your Sav - ior come,   and ____

tri - umphs   of   his   grace!
hon - ors   of   thy   name.
life,   and health, and   peace.
blood   a - vailed   for   me.
hum - ble   poor   be - lieve.
leap,   ye lame,   for   joy.

O GOD OUR HELP IN AGES PAST

words by
Isaac Watts (1674–1748), alt;
para. of Psalm 90:1-5

music by
St. Anne, melody att.
William Croft (1678-1727)
harm. William Henry Monk (1823–1889)

1. O God, our help in a - ges past, our
2. Un - der the sha - dow of Thy throne Thy
3. Be - fore the hills in or - der stood, or
4. A thou - sand a - ges in thy sight are
5. Time, like an ev - er - roll - ing stream, bears
6. O God, our help in a - ges past, our

hope for years to come, our
saints have dwelt se - cure; suf -
earth re - ceived her frame, from
like an eve - ning gone; short
all our years a - way; they
hope for years to come, be

shel - ter from the storm - y blast, and
fi - cient is Thine arm a - lone, and
ev - er - last - ing thou art God, to
as the watch that ends the night be -
fly, for - got - ten, as a dream dies
thou our guide while life shall last, and

our e - ter - nal home:
our de - fense is sure.
end - less years the same.
fore the ris - ing sun.
at the o - pening day.
our e - ter - nal home.

O HAPPY DAY
THAT FIXED MY CHOICE

words by
Philip Doddridge, 1702-1751

music from
William McDonald's
Wesleyan Sacred Harp, 1854

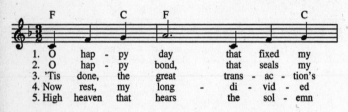

1. O hap-py day that fixed my
2. O hap-py bond, that seals my
3. 'Tis done, the great trans-ac-tion's
4. Now rest, my long di-vid-ed
5. High heaven that hears the sol-emn

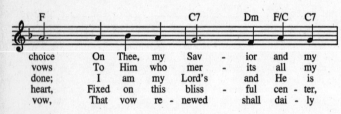

choice On Thee, my Sav-ior and my
vows To Him who mer-its all my
done; I am my Lord's and He is
heart, Fixed on this bliss-ful cen-ter,
vow, That vow re-newed shall dai-ly

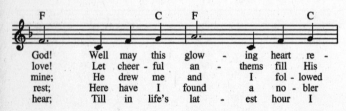

God! Well may this glow-ing heart re-
love! Let cheer-ful an-thems fill His
mine; He drew me and I fol-lowed
rest; Here have I found a no-bler
hear; Till in life's lat-est hour I

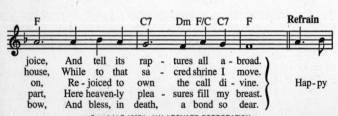

Refrain

joice, And tell its rap-tures all a-broad.
house, While to that sa-cred shrine I move.
on, Re-joiced to own the call di-vine.
part, Here heaven-ly plea-sures fill my breast.
bow, And bless, in death, a bond so dear.

Hap-py

day, hap - py day, When Je - sus

washed my sins a - way! He taught me

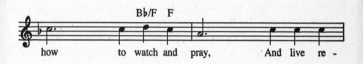

how to watch and pray, And live re -

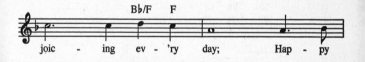

joic - ing ev - 'ry day; Hap - py

day, hap - py day, When Je - sus

washed my sins a - way!

O, HOW I LOVE JESUS

words by
Frederick Whitfield

music by
American Melody

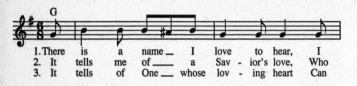

1. There is a name __ I love to hear, I
2. It tells me of __ a Sav-ior's love, Who
3. It tells of One __ whose lov-ing heart Can

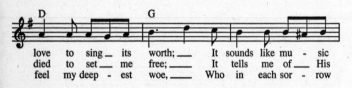

love to sing __ its worth; __ It sounds like mu - sic
died to set __ me free; __ It tells me of __ His
feel my deep - est woe, __ Who in each sor - row

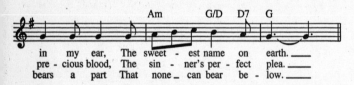

in my ear, The sweet - est name on earth. __
pre - cious blood, The sin - ner's per - fect plea. __
bears a part That none __ can bear be - low. __

O, how I love Je - sus, O, how I love

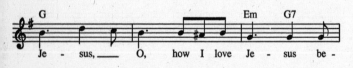

Je - sus, __ O, how I love Je - sus be -

cause __ He first loved me! __

O JESUS,
I HAVE PROMISED

words by
John E. Bode, 1868

music by
Arthur H. Mann, 1883

1. O Je - sus, I have prom - ised To serve Thee to the end; Be Thou for - ev - er near me, My Mas - ter and my Friend; I shall not fear the bat - tle If Thou art by my side, Nor wan - der from the path - way If Thou wilt be my Guide.

2. O let me feel Thee near me; The world is ev - er near! I see the sights that daz - zle, The tempt - ing sounds I hear; My foes are ev - er near me, A - round me and with - in; But, Je - sus, draw Thou near - er, And shield my soul from sin.

3. O Je - sus, Thou hast prom - ised To all who fol - low Thee That where Thou art in glo - ry There shall Thy serv - ant be; And, Je - sus, I have prom - ised To serve Thee to the end; O give me grace to fol - low My Mas - ter and my Friend.

O LOVE THAT WILT NOT LET ME GO

words by
George Matheson, 1882

music by
Albert Lister Peace, 1884

O MASTER, LET ME WALK WITH THEE

words by
Washington Gladden

music by
H. Percy Smith

1. O Mas- ter, let me walk with
2. Help me the slow of heart to
3. Teach me Thy pa- tience! Still with
4. In hope that sends a shin- ing

Thee In low- ly paths of
move By some clear, win- ning
Thee In clos- er, dear- er
ray Far down the fu- ture's

serv- ice free; Tell me Thy
word of love; Teach me the
com- pa- ny, In work that
broad- ening way, In peace that

se- cret; help me bear The
way- ward feet to stay, And
keeps faith sweet and strong, In
on- ly Thou canst give, With

strain of toil, the fret of care.
guide them in the home- ward way.
trust that tri- umphs o- ver wrong;
Thee, O Mas- ter, let me live.

O PERFECT LOVE

words by
Dorothy Frances Gurney, 1883

music by
Joseph Barnby, 1889

1. O per - fect love, all hu - man thought tran - scend - ing, Low - ly we kneel in prayer be - fore Thy throne, That theirs may be the love which knows no end - ing, Whom Thou for - ev - er - more dost join in one.

2. O per - fect life, be Thou their full as - sur - ance Of ten - der char - i - ty and stead - fast faith, Of pa - tient hope, and qui - et, brave en - dur - ance, With child - like trust that fears nor pain nor death.

3. Grant them the joy which bright - ens earth - ly sor - row; Grant them the peace which calms all earth - ly strife, And to life's day the glo - rious un - known mor - row That dawns up - on e - ter - nal love and life.

O SACRED HEAD, NOW WOUNDED

words by
Paul Gerhardt;
based on Medieval Latin poem
ascribed to Bernard of Clairvaux
translated from the German by James W. Alexander

music by
Hans Leo Hassler
harmonized by J.S. Bach

C   F   C/E   G7/B   C   F6   G   C   E7/B

1. O   sa - cred   Head,   now   wound - ed,   With
2. What   Thou,   my   Lord,   has   suf - fered   Was
3. What   lan - guage   shall   I   bor - row   To

Am   Esus   E7   Am   C   F   C/E   G7/B   C

grief   and   shame _ weighed   down,   Now   scorn - ful - ly   sur -
all   for   sin - ners'   gain;   Mine,   mine   was   the   trans -
thank   Thee,   dear - est   Friend,   For   this,   Thy   dy - ing

F6   G   C   E7/B   Am   Esus   E7   Am

round - ed   With   thorns   Thine   on - ly   crown: How
gres - sion,   But   Thine   the   dead - ly   pain.   Lo,
sor - row,   Thy   pit - y   with - out   end?   O

Dm6   Em   F   G7/D   F/C   C

pale _ Thou   art   with   an - guish,   With
here _ I   fall,   my   Sav - ior;   'Tis
make _ me   Thine   for - ev - er,   And

F   C   Dm   A   D7/F#   G   C/E   G

sore   a - buse   and   scorn,   How   does _ that   vis - age
I   de - serve   Thy   place;   Look   on _ me   with   Thy
should   I   faint - ing   be,   Lord,   let _ me   nev - er,

C6   D   G   C   F/A   C/G   F6   G   C

lan - guish,   Which   once   was   bright   as   morn!
fa - vor,   As - sist   me   with   Thy   grace.
nev - er   Out - live   my   love   to   Thee.

O WORSHIP THE KING

words by
Robert Grant (1779–1838)

music by
Hanover, att.
William Croft (1678–1727)

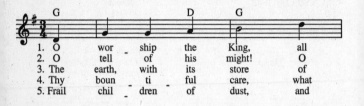

1. O wor – ship the King, all
2. O tell of his might! O
3. The earth, with its store of
4. Thy boun – ti – ful care, what
5. Frail chil – dren of dust, and

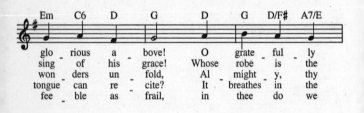

glo – rious a – bove! O grate – ful – ly
sing of his grace! Whose robe is the
won – ders un – fold, Al – might – y, thy
tongue can re – cite? It breathes in the
fee – ble as frail, in thee do we

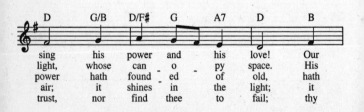

sing his power and his love! Our
light, whose can o – py space. His
power hath found – ed of old, hath
air; it shines in the light; it
trust, nor find thee to fail; thy

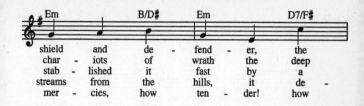

shield and de - fend - er, the
char - iots of wrath the deep
stab - lished it fast by a
streams from the hills, it de -
mer - cies, how ten - der! how

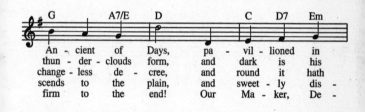

An - cient of Days, pa - vil - lioned in
thun - der - clouds form, and dark is his
change - less de - cree, and round it hath
scends to the plain, and sweet - ly dis -
firm to the end! Our Ma - ker, De -

splen - dor and gird - ed with praise.
path on the wings of the storm.
cast, like a man - tle, the sea.
tills in the dew and the rain.
fend - er, Re - deem - er, and Friend!

O ZION HASTE

words by
Mary A. Thomas, 1834–1923

music by
James Walch, 1837–1901

1. O Zi - on haste, your
2. Pub - lish to ev - 'ry
3. Give of your own to
4. He comes a - gain! O

mis - sion high ful - fill - ing,
peo - ple, tongue, and na - tion
bear the mes - sage glo - rious,
Zi - on, ere you meet him,

To tell to all the
That God, in whom they
Give of your wealth to
Make known to ev - 'ry

world that God is light;
live and move, is love;
speed them on their way,
heart his sav - ing grace;

That he who made all
Tell how he stooped to
Pour out your soul for
Let none whom he has

D · Gm

na - tions is not will - ing
save his lost cre - a - tion
them in prayer vic - to - rious,
ran - somed fail to greet him,

C7 · F/A · Dm

One soul should per - ish,
And died on earth that
And haste on the com - ing
Through your ne - glect, un -

Bb · C · F

lost in shades of night.
we might live a - bove.
of the glo - rious day.
fit to see his face.

Refrain
F7 · Bb

Pub - lish glad tid - ings,

F7 · Bb

tid - ings of peace,

G7 · Cm

Tid - ings of Je - sus, re -

Bb/F · F7 · Bb

demp - tion, and re - lease.

THE OLD
RUGGED CROSS

words by
George Bennard

music by
George Bennard

1. On a hill far a - way stood an
2. O that old rug - ged cross, so de -
3. In the old rug - ged cross, stained with
4. To the old rug - ged cross I will

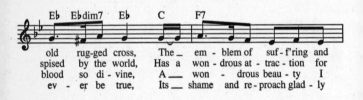

old rug-ged cross, The __ em - blem of suf - f'ring and
spised by the world, Has a won - drous at - trac - tion for
blood so di - vine, A __ won - drous beau - ty I
ev - er be true, Its __ shame and re - proach glad - ly

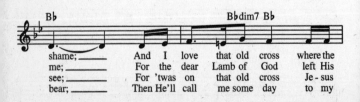

shame; _____ And I love that old cross where the
me; _____ For the dear Lamb of God left His
see; _____ For 'twas on that old cross Je - sus
bear; _____ Then He'll call me some day to my

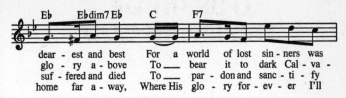

dear - est and best For a world of lost sin - ners was
glo - ry a - bove To ___ bear it to dark Cal - va -
suf - fered and died To ___ par - don and sanc - ti - fy
home far a - way, Where His glo - ry for - ev - er I'll

Refrain

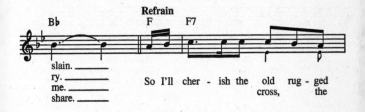

slain. ___
ry. ___
me. ___ So I'll cher - ish the old rug - ged
share. ___ cross, the

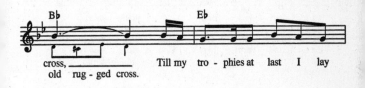

cross, ___ Till my tro - phies at last I lay
old rug - ged cross.

down; ___ I will cling to the old rug - ged
cross, the

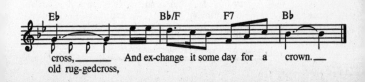

cross, ___ And ex-change it some day for a crown. ___
old rug-ged cross,

O SPIRIT OF
THE LIVING GOD

words by
James Montgomery, 1823

music from
Musikalisches Handbuch, Hamburg, 1690

1. O Spir-it of the liv-ing God, In
2. Give tongues of fire and hearts of love To
3. Be dark-ness, at your com-ing, light; Con-
4. O Spir-it of the Lord, pre-pare All
5. Bap-tize the na-tions; far and nigh The

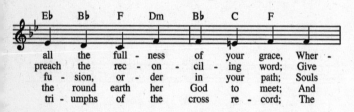

all the full - ness of your grace, Wher -
preach the rec - on - cil - ing word; Give
fu - sion, or - der in your path; Souls
the round earth her God to meet; And
tri - umphs of the cross re - cord; The

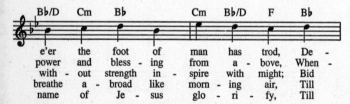

e'er the foot of man has trod, De-
power and bless - ing from a - bove, When-
with - out strength in - spire with might; Bid
breathe a - broad like morn - ing air, Till
name of Je - sus glo - ri - fy, Till

scend on our re - bel - lious race.
e'er the joy - ful sound is heard.
mer - cy tri - umph o - ver wrath.
hearts of stone be - gin to beat.
ev - ery kin - dred call him Lord.

ON JORDAN'S STORMY
BANKS I STAND

words by
Samuel Stennett, 1787

music by
American folk hymn
Arr. by Rigdon M. McIntosh, 1895

1. On __ Jor - dan's storm - y banks I stand, __ And
2. All __ o'er those wide __ ex - tend - ed plains Shines
3. No __ chill - ing winds __ nor pois - 'nous breath _ Can
4. When _ shall I reach _ that hap - py place, _ And

cast a wish - ful eye To __ Ca - naan's fair and
one e - ter - nal day; There _ God the __ Son for -
reach that health - ful shore; Sick - ness and _ sor - row,
be for - ev - er blest? When _ shall I __ see my

hap - py land, Where _ my pos - se - sions lie.
ev - er reigns And _ scat - ters _ night a - way.
pain and death Are _ felt and _ feared no more. I am
Fa - ther's face, And _ in His _ bos - som rest?

bound for the prom - ised land, I am

bound for the prom - ised land; O who will come and

go with me? I am bound for the prom - ised land.

ONCE TO EVERY MAN AND NATION

words by
James Russel Lowell

music by
Thomas J. Williams

1. Once to ev-ery man and na-tion Comes the mo-ment to de-cide. In the strife of truth with false-hood, For the good or e-vil side. Some great cause, some great de-ci-sion, Of-f'ring each the bloom or blight, And the choice goes by for-ev-er 'Twixt that dark-ness and that light.

2. Then to side with truth is no-ble, When we share her wretch-ed crust. Ere her cause bring fame and prof-it, And 'tis pros-p'rous to be just. Then it is the brave man choos-es While the cow-ard stands a-side, Til the mul-ti-tude make vir-tue Of the faith they had de-nied.

3. Though the cause of e-vil pros-per, Yet the truth a-lone is strong. Though her por-tion be the scaf-fold, And up-on the throne be wrong. Yet that scaf-fold sways the fu-ture, And, be-hind the dim un-known, Stand-eth God with-in the shad-ow, Keep-ing watch a-bove His own.

ONLY TRUST HIM

words by
John H. Stockton

music by
John H. Stockton

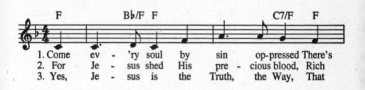

1. Come ev - 'ry soul by sin op-pressed There's
2. For Je - sus shed His pre - cious blood, Rich
3. Yes, Je - sus is the Truth, the Way, That

mer - cy with the Lord, And He will sure - ly
bless - ings to be - stow; Plunge now in - to the
leads you in - to rest: Be - lieve in Him with -

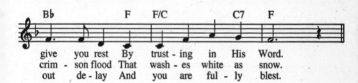

give you rest By trust - ing in His Word.
crim - son flood That wash - es white as snow.
out de - lay And you are ful - ly blest.

Refrain

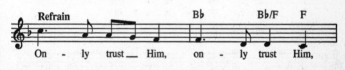

On - ly trust __ Him, on - ly trust Him,

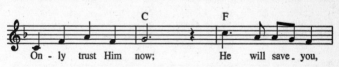

On - ly trust Him now; He will save __ you,

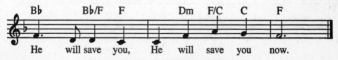

He will save you, He will save you now.

174

ONWARD CHRISTIAN SOLDIERS

words by
Sabine Baring-Gould

music by
Arthur S. Sullivan

1. On - ward, Chris - tian sol - diers,
2. At the sign of tri - umph
3. Like a might - y ar - my
4. On - ward, then, ye peo - ple,

March - ing as to war,
Sa - tan's host doth flee;
Moves the Church of God;
Join our hap - py throng;

With the cross of Je - sus
On, then, Chris - tian sol - diers,
Broth - ers, we are tread - ing
Blend with ours your voic - es

Go - ing on be - fore!
On to vic - to - ry!
Where the saints have trod.
In the tri - umph song.

Christ, the roy - al Mas - ter,
Hell's foun - da - tions quiv - er
We are not di - vid - ed,
Glo - ry, laud and hon - or

Leads a - gainst the foe;
At the shout of praise;
All one bod - y we
Un - to Christ the King

175

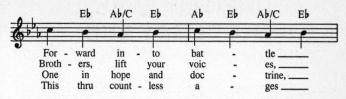

For - ward in - to bat - tle ____
Broth - ers, lift your voic - es, ____
One in hope and doc - trine, ____
This thru count - less a - ges ____

See His ban - ners go!
Loud your an - thems raise!
One in char - i - ty.
Men and an - gels sing.

Refrain

On - ward, Chris - tian sol - diers, ____

march - ing as to ____ war,

With the cross of Je - sus

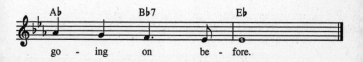

go - ing on be - fore.

OPEN MY EYES,
THAT I MAY SEE

words by
Clara H. Scott, 1895

music by
Clara H. Scott, 1895

1. O- pen my eyes, that I may see
2. O- pen my ears, that I may hear
3. O- pen my mouth, and let me bear

Glimps- es of truth Thou hast for me;
Voic- es of truth Thou send - est clear;
Glad- ly the warm truth ev - ery - where;

Place in my hands the won- der - ful key
And while the wave notes fall on my ear,
O- pen my heart, and let me pre - pare

That shall un - clasp and set me free.
Ev - ery - thing false will dis - ap - pear.
Love with Thy chil - dren thus to share.

Refrain

Si- lent- ly now I wait for Thee. Read- y, my God. Thy

will to see: O- pen my ears, il -
eyes.
heart.

lu - mine me. Spir - it di - vine! ____

PASS ME NOT, O GENTLE SAVIOR

words by
Fanny J. Crosby

music by
William H. Doane

1. Pass me not, O gen - tle Sav - ior
2. Let me at a throne of mer - cy
3. Trust - ing on - ly in Thy mer - it,
4. Thou the spring of all my com - fort,

Hear my hum - ble cry! While on oth - ers Thou art
Find a sweet re - lief; Kneel - ing there in deep con -
Would I seek Thy face; Heal my wound-ed, bro - ken
More than life to me! Whom have I on earth be -

call - ing, Do not pass me by.
tri - tion Help my un - be - lief.
spir - it, Save me by thy grace.
side Thee? Whom in heav'n but Thee?

Refrain

Sav - ior, Sav - ior, Hear my hum - ble

cry! While on oth - ers Thou art

call - ing, Do not pass me by.

THE PALMS

words by
Adapt. by Charles H. Gabriel,
1856–1932

music by
J. Baptiste Faure, 1830–1914
Arr. by Charles H. Gabriel, 1856-1932

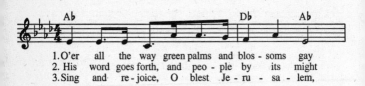

1. O'er all the way green palms and blos - soms gay
2. His word goes forth, and peo - ple by its might
3. Sing and re - joice, O blest Je - ru - sa - lem,

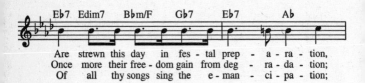

Are strewn this day in fes - tal prep - a - ra - tion,
Once more their free - dom gain from deg - ra - da - tion;
Of all thy songs sing the e - man - ci - pa - tion;

Where Je - sus comes, to wipe our tears a - way;
Hu - man - i - ty doth give to each his right,
Through bound - less love, the Christ of Beth - le - hem

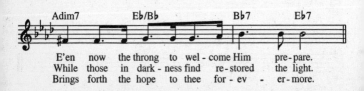

E'en now the throng to wel - come Him pre - pare.
While those in dark - ness find re - stored the light.
Brings forth the hope to thee for - ev - er - more.

Refrain

Join all, and sing Ho - san - na!

Let ev - ery voice re - sound with u -

nit - ed ac - cla - ma - tion, Ho -

san - na! Praised be the Lord,

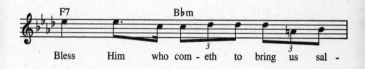

Bless Him who com - eth to bring us sal -

va - tion.

PRAISE GOD FROM WHOM ALL BLESSINGS FLOW

words by
Thomas Ken, 1674

music by
Attr. to Louis Bourgeois, 1551

Praise God, from whom all bless- ings

flow; praise him, all crea-tures here be - low; praise

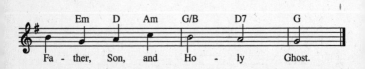

him a-bove, ye heaven - ly host; praise

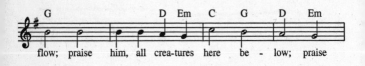

Fa - ther, Son, and Ho - ly Ghost.

PRAISE TO THE
LIVING GOD

words by
Medieval Jewish liturgy
tr. Max Landsberg (1845-1928)
and Newton M. Mann (1836-1926)

music by
Leoni, Hebrew melody
harm. *Hymns Ancient and Modern,*
1875, alt.

1. Praise to the liv-ing God! All prais-ed be his Name who was, and is, and is to be, for ay the same. The one e-ter-nal God ere aught that now ap-pears: the first, the last, be-yond all thought his time-less years!

2. Form-less, all love-ly forms de-clare his lov-li-ness; ho-ly, no ho-li-ness of earth can his ex-press. Lo, he is Lord of all. Cre-a-tion speaks his praise, and ev-ery-where a-bove, be-low, his will o-beys.

3. His Spi-rit flow-eth free, high surg-ing where it will; in pro-phet's word he spoke of old; he speak-eth still. Es-tab-lished is his law, and change-less it shall stand, deep writ up-on the hu-man heart, on sea, on land.

4. E-ter-nal life hath he im-plant-ed in the soul; his love shall be our strength and stay while a-ges roll. Praise to the liv-ing God! All prais-ed be his Name who was, and is, and is to be, for ay the same.

PRAISE TO THE LORD, THE ALMIGHTY

words by
Joachim Neander, 1680

music by
Erneuerten Gesangbuch, 1665

sts. 1,3,5 trans. by
Catherine Winkworth, 1863

harm. by
William Sterndale Bennett, 1864

st. 4 by Rupert E. Davies, 1983 (Ps. 103:1-6; 150)

1. Praise to the Lord, the Al-might-y, the King of cre-a - tion! O my soul, praise him, for he is thy health and sal - va - tion! All ye who hear, now to his tem - ple draw near; join me in glad ad - o - ra - tion!

2. Praise to the Lord, who o'er all things so won-drous-ly reign - ing bears thee on ea - gle's wings, e'er in his keep-ing main-tain - ing. God's care - en - folds all, whose true good he up-holds. Hast thou not known his sus - tain - ing?

3. Praise to the Lord, who doth pros-per thy work and de - fend thee; sure - ly his good - ness and mer - cy here dai - ly at - tend thee. Pon - der a - new what the Al - might - y can do, who with his love doth be - friend thee.

4. Praise to the Lord, who doth nour-ish thy life and re - store thee, fit - ting thee well for the tasks that are ev - er be - fore thee. Then to thy need God as a moth - er doth speed, spread-ing the wings of grace o'er thee.

5. Praise to the Lord! O let all that is in me a - dore him! All that hath life and breath, come now with prais - es be - fore him! Let the a - men sound from his peo - ple a - gain; glad - ly for - ev - er a - dore him.

REJOICE YE PURE IN HEART

words by
Edward Hayes Plumptre, 1865

music by
Arthur Henry Messiter, 1883

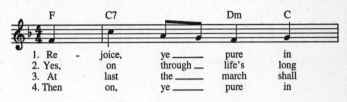

1. Re - joice, ye _____ pure in
2. Yes, on through _ life's long
3. At last the _____ march shall
4. Then on, ye pure in

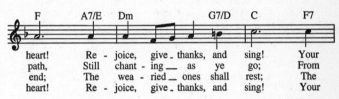

heart! Re - joice, give _ thanks, and sing! Your
path, Still chant - ing _ as ye go; From
end; The wea - ried _ ones shall rest; The
heart! Re - joice, give _ thanks, and sing! Your

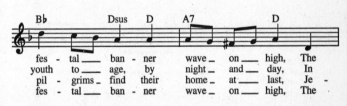

fes - tal _ ban - ner wave on _ high, The
youth to _ age, by night _ and day, In
pil - grims _ find their home _ at _ last, Je -
fes - tal _ ban - ner wave _ on _ high, The

Refrain

cross of Christ your King.
glad - ness and in woe. Re - joice! re -
ru - sa - lem the blest.
cross of Christ your King.

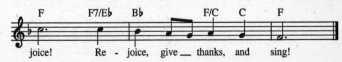

joice! Re - joice, give _ thanks, and sing!

REDEEMED

words by
Fanny J. Crosby

music by
William J. Kirkpatrick

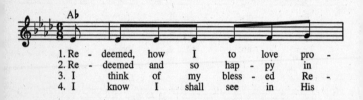

1. Re - deemed, how I to love pro -
2. Re - deemed and so hap - py in
3. I think of my bless - ed Re -
4. I know I shall see in His

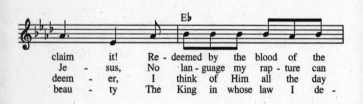

claim it! Re - deemed by the blood of the
Je - sus, No lan - guage my rap - ture can
deem - er, I think of Him all the day
beau - ty The King in whose law I de -

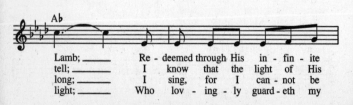

Lamb; _____ Re - deemed through His in - fin - ite
tell; _____ I know that the light of His
long; _____ I sing, for I can - not be
light; _____ Who lov - ing - ly guard - eth my

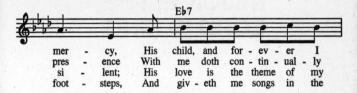

mer - cy, His child, and for - ev - er I
pres - ence With me doth con - tin - ual - ly
si - lent; His love is the theme of my
foot - steps, And giv - eth me songs in the

Refrain

am. _____
dwell. _____
song. _____
night. _____

Re - deemed, _____ re -

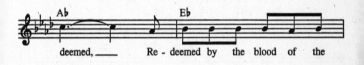

deemed, _____ Re - deemed by the blood of the

Lamb; _____ Re - deemed, _____ re -

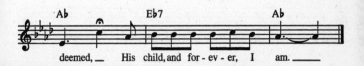

deemed, ___ His child, and for - ev - er, I am. _____

REJOICE, THE LORD IS KING

words by
Charles Wesley, 1746

music by
John Darwall, 1770

1. Re - joice, the Lord is King! Your
2. God's king - dom can - not fail, Christ
3. Re - joice in glo - rious hope! For

Lord and King a - dore! Re - joice, give thanks, and
rules o'er earth and heaven; The keys of death and
Christ, the Judge, shall come To glo - ri - fy the

sing, And tri - umph ev - er - more: Lift
hell Are to our Je - sus given: Lift
saints For their e - ter - nal home:

up your heart, lift up your voice! Re -

joice, a - gain I say, re - joice!

RESCUE THE PERISHING

words by
Fanny J. Crosby

music by
William H. Doane

1. Res - cue the per - ish - ing, care for the dy - ing,
2. Tho they are slight-ing Him, still He is wait - ing,
3. Down in the hu - man heart, crushed by the tempt - er,
4. Res - cue the per - ish - ing, du - ty de - mands it

Snatch them in pit - y from sin and the grave;
Wait - ing the pen - i - tent child to re - ceive;
Feel - ings lie bur - ied that grace can re - store;
Strength for your la - bor the Lord will pro - vide;

Weep o'er the err - ing one, lift up the fall - en,
Plead with them ear - nest - ly, plead with them gen - tly,
Touched by a lov - ing heart, wak - ened by kind - ness,
Back to the nar - row way pa - tient - ly win them,

Tell them of Je - sus, the might - y to save.
He will for - give if they on - ly be - lieve.
Cords that are bro - ken will vi - brate once more.
Tell the poor wan - d'rer a Sav - ior has died.

Refrain

Res - cue the per - ish - ing, Care for the dy - ing;

Je - sus is mer - ci - ful, Je - sus will save.

RISE UP, O MEN
OF GOD

words by
William Pierson Merrill, 1911, 1972

music by
William H. Walter, 1894

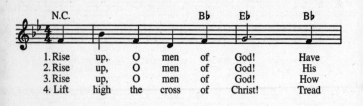

1. Rise up, O men of God! Have
2. Rise up, O men of God! His
3. Rise up, O men of God! How
4. Lift high the cross of Christ! Tread

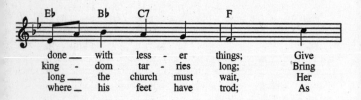

done _ with less - er things; Give
king - dom tar - ries long; Bring
long _ the church must wait, Her
where _ his feet have trod; As

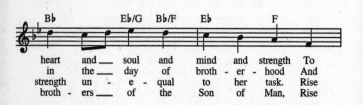

heart and _ soul and mind and strength To
in the _ day of broth - er - hood And
strength un - e - qual to her task. Rise
broth - ers _ of the Son of Man, Rise

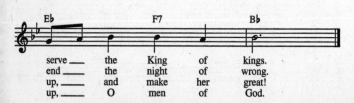

serve _ the King of kings.
end _ the night of wrong.
up, _ and make her great!
up, _ O men of God.

ROCK OF AGES

words by
Augustus M. Toplady

music by
Thomas Hastings

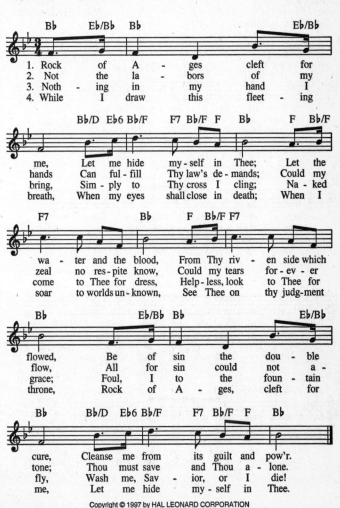

1. Rock of A - ges cleft for me, Let me hide my-self in Thee; Let the wa - ter and the blood, From Thy riv - en side which flowed, Be of sin the dou - ble cure, Cleanse me from its guilt and pow'r.

2. Not the la - bors of my hands Can ful - fill Thy law's de - mands; Could my zeal no res - pite know, Could my tears for - ev - er flow, All for sin could not a - tone; Thou must save and Thou a - lone.

3. Noth - ing in my hand I bring, Sim - ply to Thy cross I cling; Na - ked come to Thee for dress, Help - less, look to Thee for grace; Foul, I to the foun - tain fly, Wash me, Sav - ior, or I die!

4. While I draw this fleet - ing breath, When my eyes shall close in death; When I soar to worlds un - known, See Thee on thy judg - ment throne, Rock of A - ges, cleft for me, Let me hide my - self in Thee.

SAVIOR LIKE A
SHEPHERD LEAD US

words by
Hymns for the Young, 1836;
attributed to Dorothy A. Thrupp

music by
William B. Bradbury

1. Sav - ior, like a shep - herd lead ___ us, ___
2. We are Thine; do Thou be - friend ___ us, ___
3. Thou hast prom-ised to re - ceive ___ us, ___
4. Ear - ly let us seek Thy fa - vor; ___

Much we need Thy ten - der care;
Be the Guard - ian of our way;
Poor and sin - ful though we be;
Ear - ly let us do Thy will;

In Thy pleas - ant pas - tures feed ___ us, ___
Keep Thy flock, from sin de - fend ___ us, ___
Thou hast mer - cy to re - lieve ___ us, ___
Bless - ed Lord and on - ly Sav - ior,

For our use Thy folds pre - pare: Bless - ed
Seek us when we go a - stray: Bless - ed
Grace to cleanse, and pow'r to free: Bless - ed
With Thy love our bos - oms fill: Bless - ed

	Gb				Db	
Je -	sus,	bless - ed	Je -	sus,	Thou	hast
Je -	sus,	bless - ed	Je -	sus,	Hear,	O
Je -	sus,	bless - ed	Je -	sus,	Ear -	ly
Je -	sus,	bless - ed	Je -	sus,	Thou	hast

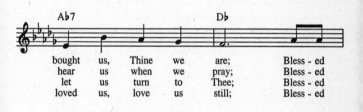

Ab7					Db	
bought	us,	Thine	we	are;	Bless - ed	
hear	us	when	we	pray;	Bless - ed	
let	us	turn	to	Thee;	Bless - ed	
loved	us,	love	us	still;	Bless - ed	

Gb				Db		Gb6/Db
Je - sus,	bless - ed	Je -	sus,	Thou hast		
Je - sus,	bless - ed	Je -	sus,	Hear, O		
Je - sus,	bless - ed	Je -	sus,	Ear - ly		
Je - sus,	bless - ed	Je -	sus,	Thou hast		

Db		Ab7		Db
bought	us,	Thine	we	are.
hear	us	when	we	pray.
let	us	turn	to	Thee.
loved	us,	love	us	still.

SHALL I CRUCIFY
MY SAVIOR?

words by
Carrie Breck, 1896

music by
Grant Colfax Tullar, 1896

1. Shall I cru - ci - fy my Sav - ior,
2. Are temp - ta - tions so al - lur - ing?
3. 'Twas my sins that cru - ci - fied ____ Him:
4. Oh, the kind - ly hands of Je - sus,

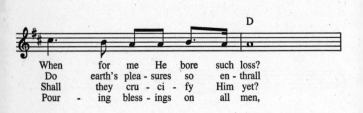

When for me He bore such loss?
Do earth's plea - sures so en - thrall
Shall they cru - ci - fy Him yet?
Pour - ing bless - ings on all men,

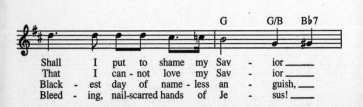

Shall I put to shame my Sav - ior ____
That I can - not love my Sav - ior ____
Black - est day of name - less an - guish, ____
Bleed - ing, nail-scarred hands of Je - sus! ____

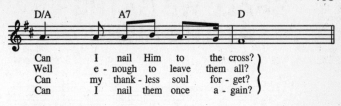

Can   I   nail   Him   to   the cross?
Well   e - nough them   leave them all?
Can   my thank - less soul   for - get?
Can   I   nail   them once   a - gain?

Refrain

Shall   I   cru - ci - fy   my   Sa -   vior?

Cru - ci - fy   my   Lord   a - gain? _____

Once,   oh   once, I   cru - ci - fied   Him: _____

Shall   I   cru - ci - fy   a - gain?

SHALL WE GATHER AT THE RIVER

words by
Robert Lowry

music by
Robert Lowry

1. Shall we gath - er at the riv - er
2. Ere we reach the shin - ing riv - er,
3. Soon we'll reach the shin - ing riv - er;

Where bright an - gel feet have trod, ____
Lay we ev - 'ry bur - den down; ____
Soon our pil - grim-age will cease; ____

With its crys - tal tide for - ev - er Flow - ing
Grace our spir - its will de - liv - er And pro -
Soon our hap - py hearts will quiv - er With the

by the throne of __ God?
vide us a robe and a crown.
mel - o - dy of __ peace.

Yes, we'll gath - er at the

riv - er, The beau - ti - ful, the beau - ti - ful ___

riv - er, Gath - er with the saints __ at the

riv - er That flows by the throne of __ God.

SPIRIT DIVINE, ATTEND OUR PRAYERS

words by
Andrew Reed, 1829

music by
Crüger's *Praxis Pietatis Melica, 1653*

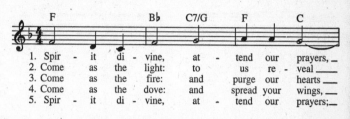

1. Spir - it di - vine, at - tend our prayers, _
2. Come as the light: to us re - veal _
3. Come as the fire: and purge our hearts _
4. Come as the dove: and spread your wings, _
5. Spir - it di - vine, at - tend our prayers; _

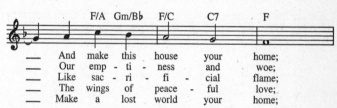

_ And make this house your home;
_ Our emp - ti - ness and woe;
_ Like sac - ri - fi - cial flame;
_ The wings of peace - ful love;
_ Make a lost world your home;

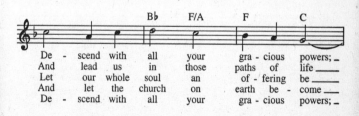

De - scend with all your gra - cious powers;
And lead us in those paths of life _
Let our whole soul an of - fering be _
And let the church on earth be - come _
De - scend with all your gra - cious powers;

_ O come, great Spir - it, come!
_ Where all the right - eous go.
_ To our re - deem - er's name.
_ Blest as the church a - bove.
_ O come, great Spir - it, come!

SOFTLY AND TENDERLY

words by
Will L. Thompson

music by
Will L. Thompson

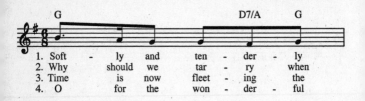

G   D7/A   G

1. Soft - ly and ten - der - ly
2. Why should we tar - ry when
3. Time is now fleet - ing the
4. O for the won - der - ful

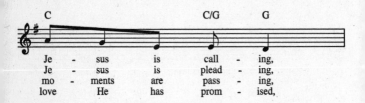

C   C/G   G

Je - sus is call - ing,
Je - sus is plead - ing,
mo - ments are pass - ing,
love He has prom - ised,

            A7/E   D

Call - ing for you and for me; _____
Plead - ing for you and for me? _____
Pass - ing from you and from me; _____
Prom - ised for you and for me! _____

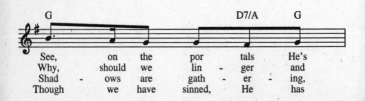

G   D7/A   G

See, on the por - tals He's
Why, should we lin - ger and
Shad - ows are gath - er - ing,
Though we have sinned, He has

197

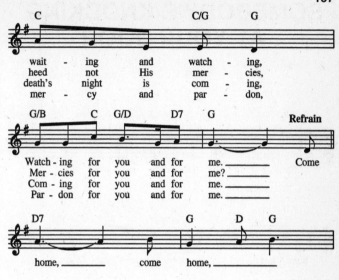

wait - ing and watch - ing,
heed not His mer - cies,
death's night is com - ing,
mer - cy and par - don,

Watch - ing for you and for me. _____ Come
Mer - cies for you and for me? _____
Com - ing for you and for me. _____
Par - don for you and for me. _____

home, _____ come home, _____

Ye who are wea - ry, come home; _____

Ear - nest-ly, ten - der - ly, Je - sus is call - ing,

Call-ing, O sin - ner, come home! _____

SOMEBODY'S KNOCKING AT YOUR DOOR

African-American Spiritual

Some - bod - y's knock - ing at your door,

Some - bod - y's knock - ing at your door.

O _____ sin - ner, why don't you

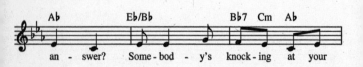

an - swer? Some - bod - y's knock - ing at your

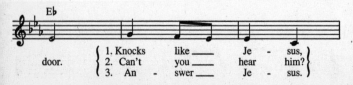

door.
{ 1. Knocks like _____ Je - sus, }
{ 2. Can't you _____ hear him? }
{ 3. An - swer _____ Je - sus. }

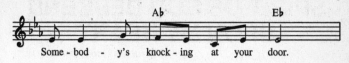

Some - bod - y's knock - ing at your door.

{ Knocks like ___ Je - sus, }
{ Can't you ___ hear him? }   Some - bod - y's
(An - swer ___ Je - sus.)

knock - ing at your door.   O ___

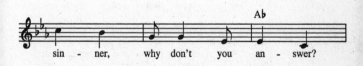

sin - ner, why don't you an - swer?

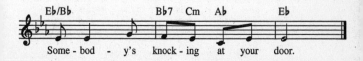

Some - bod - y's knock - ing at your door.

SPIRIT OF GOD DESCEND UPON MY HEART

words by
George Croly, 1854

music by
Frederick Cook Atkinson, 1870

C   G7/B   C

1. Spir - it of God, de -
2. Hast Thou not bid us
3. Teach me to feel that
4. Teach me to love Thee

F   C/E   Dm7   G7   C   Am   B

scend up - on my heart; Wean it from
love Thee, God and King; All, all Thine
Thou art al - ways nigh; Teach me the
as Thine an - gels love, One ho - ly

Em   A7/E   G/D   C6/D   D7

earth, through all its puls - es and
own: soul, heart, and strength, and
strug - gles of the soul to
pas - sion fill - ing all my

G   G7   F/G

move; Stoop to my weak - ness,
mind? I see Thy cross, there
bear, To check the ris - ing
frame; The bap - tism of the

G7   C   G7/D   C/E

might - y as Thou art, And make me
teach my heart to cling. O let me
doubt, the reb - el sigh; Teach me the
heaven - de - scend - ed Dove, My heart an

F   C/G   F/A   C/G   G7   C

love Thee as I ought to love.
seek Thee, and O let me find!
pa - tience of un - an - swered prayer.
al - tar, and Thy love the flame.

STAND UP AND BLESS THE LORD

words by
James Montgomery (Neh. 9:5)

music by
Genevan Psalter, 1551;
adapt. by William Crotch, 1836

1. Stand up and bless the Lord, ye peo - ple of his choice; stand up and bless the Lord your God with heart and soul and voice.

2. Though high a - bove all praise, a - bove all bless - ing high, who would not fear his ho - ly name, and laud and mag - ni - fy?

3. O for the liv - ing flame from his own al - tar brought, to touch our lips our minds in - spire, and wing to heaven our thought!

4. God is our strength and song, and his sal - va - tion ours; then be his love in Christ pro - claimed with all our ran - somed powers.

5. Stand up and bless the Lord; the Lord your God a - dore; stand up and bless his glo - rious name, hence - forth for - ev - er more.

STAND UP, STAND UP FOR JESUS

words by
George Duffield, Jr.

music by
George J. Webb

1. Stand up, stand up for Je - sus, Ye sol - diers of the cross, List high His roy - al ban - ner, It must not suf - fer loss; From vic - tory un - to vic - tory His ar - my shall He lead, ___ Till ev - ery foe is van - quished And Christ is Lord in - deed.

2. Stand up, stand up for Je - sus, The trum - pet call o - bey; Forth to the might - y con - flict In this His glo - rious day, Ye that are men, now serve Him A - gainst un - num - bered foes; ___ Let cour - age rise with dan - ger, And strength to strength op - pose.

3. Stand up, stand up for Je - sus, Stand in His strength a - lone; The arm of flesh will fail you Ye dare not trust your own; Put on the gos - pel ar - mor, Each piece put on with prayer; ___ Where du - ty calls, or dan - ger, Be nev - er want - ing there.

4. Stand up, stand up for Je - sus, The bat - tle, The next, the vic - tor's song; To strife will not be long; This day the noise of him who o - ver - com - eth A crown of life shall be; ___ He with the King of glo - ry Shall reign e - ter - nal - ly.

THE STRIFE IS O'ER, THE BATTLE DONE

words by
Symphonia Sirenum, *Köln*, 1695;
tr. Francis Pott, 1832-1909

music by
Giovanni P. da Palestrina
1525–1594, adapt.

Al - le - lu - ia, al - le - lu - ia, al - le - lu -

ia!

1. The strife is o'er, the bat - tle
2. The pow'rs of death have done their
3. The three sad days have quick - ly
4. He broke the age - bound chains of
5. Lord, by the stripes which wound - ed

done; Now is the vic - tor's tri - umph
worst, But Christ their le - gions has dis -
sped, He ris - es glo - rious from the
hell; The bars from heav'n's high por - tals
you, From death's sting free your serv - ants

won! Now be the song of praise be -
persed. Let shouts of ho - ly joy out -
dead. All glo - ry to our ris - en
fell. Let hymns of praise his tri - umph
too, That we may live and sing to

gun, Al - le - lu - ia! Al - le - lu -
burst. Al - le - lu - ia!
head! Al - le - lu - ia!
tell. Al - le - lu - ia!
you. Al - le - lu - ia!

ia, al - le - lu - ia, al - le - lu - ia!

STANDING ON THE PROMISES

words by
R. Kelso Carter

music by
R. Kelso Carter

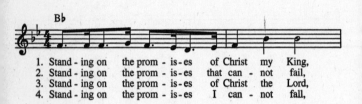

Bb

1. Stand - ing on the prom - is - es of Christ my King,
2. Stand - ing on the prom - is - es that can - not fail,
3. Stand - ing on the prom - is - es of Christ the Lord,
4. Stand - ing on the prom - is - es I can - not fall,

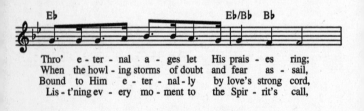

Eb   Eb/Bb   Bb

Thro' e - ter - nal a - ges let His prais - es ring;
When the howl - ing storms of doubt and fear as - sail,
Bound to Him e - ter - nal - ly by love's strong cord,
Lis - t'ning ev - ery mo - ment to the Spir - it's call,

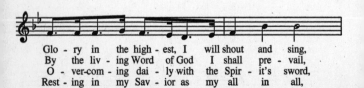

Glo - ry in the high - est, I will shout and sing,
By the liv - ing Word of God I shall pre - vail,
O - ver - com - ing dai - ly with the Spir - it's sword,
Rest - ing in my Sav - ior as my all in all,

Stand - ing on the prom - is - es of God.

Refrain

Stand - ing, stand - ing,

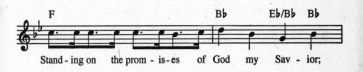

Stand - ing on the prom - is - es of God my Sav - ior;

Stand - ing, stand - ing, I'm

stand - ing on the prom - is - es of God.

SWEET HOUR OF PRAYER

words by
William W. Walford

music by
William B. Bradbury

1. Sweet hour of prayer, sweet hour of prayer, That
2. Sweet hour of prayer, sweet hour of prayer, Thy

calls me from a world of care, And bids me at my
wings shall my pe - ti - tion bear To Him whose truth and

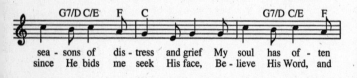

Fa - ther's throne Make all my wants and wish - es known: In
faith - ful - ness En - gage the wait - ing soul to bless: And

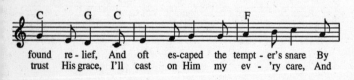

sea - sons of dis - tress and grief My soul has of - ten
since He bids me seek His face, Be - lieve His Word, and

found re - lief, And oft es - caped the tempt - er's snare By
trust His grace, I'll cast on Him my ev - 'ry care, And

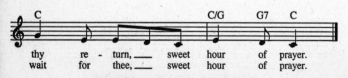

thy re - turn, ___ sweet hour of prayer.
wait for thee, ___ sweet hour of prayer.

TAKE MY LIFE
AND LET IT BE

words by
Frances R. Havergal, 1873 (Rom. 12:1)

music by
Louis J.F. Hërold, 1839
arr. by George Kingsley, 1839

1. Take my life, and let it be con - se - cra - ted,
2. Take my voice, and let me sing, al - ways, on - ly,
3. Take my will, and make it thine; it shall be no

Lord, to thee. Take my mo - ments and my days;
for my King. Take my lips, and let them be
long - er mine. Take my heart, it is thine own;

let them flow in cease - less praise. Take my hands, and
filled with mes - sag - es from thee. Take my sil - ver
it shall be thy roy - al throne. Take my love, my

let them move at the im - pulse of thy love.
and my gold; not a mite would I with - hold.
Lord, I pour at thy feet its trea - sure-store.

Take my feet, and let them be
Take my in - tel - lect, and use
Take my - self, and I will be

swift and beau - ti - ful for thee.
ev - ery power as thou shalt choose.
ev - er, on - ly, all for thee.

TAKE THE NAME OF JESUS WITH YOU

words by
Mrs. Lydia Baxter

music by
W. H. Doane

1. Take the name of Je - sus with you, Child of sor - row and of
2. Take the name of Je - sus ev - er As a shield from ev - 'ry
3. O the precious name of Je - sus! How it thrills our souls with
4. At the name of Je - sus bow - ing, Fall - ing pros - trate at His

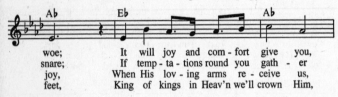

woe; It will joy and com - fort give you,
snare; If temp - ta - tions round you gath - er
joy, When His lov - ing arms re - ceive us,
feet, King of kings in Heav'n we'll crown Him,

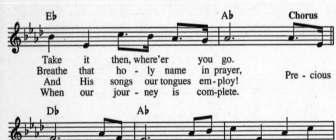

Take it then, where'er you go.
Breathe that ho - ly name in prayer,
And His songs our tongues em - ploy!
When our jour - ney is com - plete.

Chorus

Pre - cious

name, O how sweet! Hope of earth and joy of

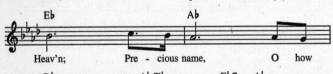

Heav'n; Pre - cious name, O how

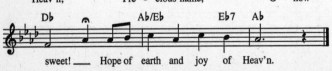

sweet! __ Hope of earth and joy of Heav'n.

TAKE TIME TO BE HOLY

words by
William D. Longstaff

music by
George C. Stebbins

1. Take time to be ho - ly, Speak oft with thy
2. Take time to be ho - ly, The world rush - es
3. Take time to be ho - ly, Let Him be thy
4. Take time to be ho - ly, Be calm in thy

Lord; _____ A - bide in Him al - ways,
on; _____ Much time spend in se - cret
guide, _____ And run not be - fore Him
soul; _____ Each thought and each mo - tive

And feed on His Word. _____ Make friends of God's
With Je - sus a - lone; _____ By look - ing to
What - ev - er be - tide; _____ In joy or in
Be - neath His con - trol; _____ Thus led by His

chil - dren; Help those who are weak; _____
Je - sus, Like Him thou shalt be; _____
sor - row Still fol - low thy Lord, _____
Spir - it To foun - tains of love, _____

For - get - ting in noth - ing
Thy friends in thy con - duct
And, look - ing to Je - sus,
Thou soon shalt be fit - ted

His bless - ing to seek. _____
His like - ness shall see. _____
Still trust in His Word. _____
For ser - vice a - bove. _____

THERE IS A FOUNTAIN

words by
William Cowper

music by
Traditional American melody;
arr. by Lowell Mason

1. There is a foun-tain filled with blood Drawn from Im-man-uel's veins, And sin-ners plunged be-neath that flood Lose all their guilt-y stains:
2. The dy-ing thief re-joiced to see That foun-tain in his day, And there may I, though vile as he, Wash all my sins a-way:
3. Dear dy-ing Lamb, Thy pre-cious blood Shall nev-er lose its pow'r, Till all the ran-somed Church of God Be saved to sin no more:
4. E're since by faith I saw the stream Thy flow-ing wounds sup-ply Re-deem-ing love has been my theme And shall be till I die:
5. When this poor lisp-ing, stam-m'ring tongue Lies si-lent in the grave, Then in a no-bler, sweet-er song I'll sing Thy pow'r to save:

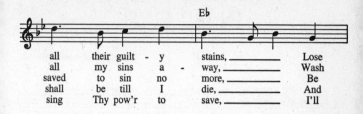

all their guilt - y stains, _____ Lose
all my sins a - way, _____ Wash
saved to sin no more, _____ Be
shall be till I die, _____ And
sing Thy pow'r to save, _____ I'll

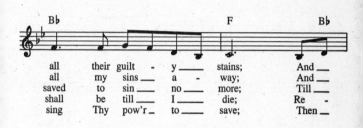

all their guilt - y _____ stains; And _____
all my sins _____ a - way; And _____
saved to sin _____ no _____ more; Till _____
shall be till I _____ die; Re -
sing Thy pow'r _ to _____ save; Then _____

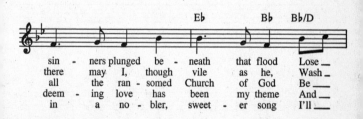

sin - ners plunged be - neath that flood Lose _____
there may I, though vile as he, Wash _____
all the ran - somed Church of God Be _____
deem - ing love has been my theme And _____
in a no - bler, sweet - er song I'll _____

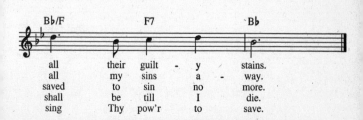

all their guilt - y stains.
all my sins a - way.
saved to sin no more.
shall be till I die.
sing Thy pow'r to save.

THERE IS A BALM IN GILEAD

African-American Spiritual

There_ is a balm in Gil - e - ad To make the wound - ed whole,_ There_ is a balm in Gil - e - ad To heal the sin - sick soul.

Fine

{ 1. Some _
{ 2. Don't_
{ 3. If you

times I feel dis - cour - aged, And __
ev - er feel dis - cour - aged, For __
can - not preach like Pe - ter, If you

think my work's in vain, But _ then the Ho - ly
Je - sus is your friend, And _ if you lack for
can - not pray like Paul, You can tell the love of

D.C.

Spir - it Re - vives my soul a - gain. __
know - ledge, He'll not re - fuse to lend. __
Je - sus And say, "He died for all." __

THERE IS A GREEN HILL
FAR AWAY

words by
Cecil Frances Alexander
(1818–1895), alt.

music by
Horsley,
William Horsley (1774–1858)

1. There is a green hill far a-way, out-
2. We may not know, we can-not tell, what
3. He died that we might be for-given, he
4. There was no o-ther good e-nough to
5. O dear-ly, dear-ly has he loved! And

side a ci-ty wall, Where
pains he had to bear, But
died to make us good, That
pay the price of sin, He
we must love him too, And

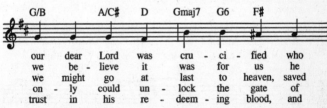

our dear Lord was cru-ci-fied who
we be-lieve it was for us he
we might go at last to heaven, saved
on-ly could un-lock the gate of
trust in his re-deem-ing blood, and

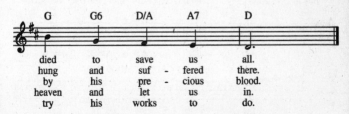

died to save us all.
hung and suf-fered there.
by his pre-cious blood.
heaven and let us in.
try his works to do.

THERE IS POWER IN THE BLOOD

words by
Lewis E. Jones, 1899

music by
Lewis E. Jones, 1899

1. Would you be free from the bur - den of sin? There's
2. Would you be free from your pas - sion and pride? There's
3. Would you be whit - er, much whit - er than snow? There's
4. Would you do ser - vice for Je - sus your King? There's

pow'r in the blood, pow'r in the blood;
pow'r in the blood, pow'r in the blood;
pow'r in the blood, pow'r in the blood;
pow'r in the blood, pow'r in the blood;

Would you o'er e - vil a vic - to - ry win? There's
Come for a cleans - ing to Cal - va - ry's tide; There's
Sin stains are lost in its life giv - ing flow; There's
Would you live dai - ly His prais - es to sing There's

Refrain

won - der - ful pow'r in the blood. There is

pow'r, pow'r, Wond - er - work - ing pow'r In the

blood of the Lamb; There is pow'r, pow'r,

Won - der - work - ing pow'r In the pre - cious blood of the Lamb.

THERE'S A WIDENESS IN GOD'S MERCY

words by
Frederick William Faber, 1854

music by
Dutch melody
Arr. Julius Röntgen (1855–1933)

1. There's a ___ wide - ness in God's mer - cy,
2. For the ___ love of God is ___ broad - er

Like the wide - ness of ___ the ___ sea; There's a ___ kind - ness
Than the mea - sures of ___ the mind; And the heart of

in God's jus - tice, Which is ___ more than ___ lib - er - ty.
the E - ter - nal Is most won - der - ful - ly kind.

There is ___ no place where earth's sor - rows
If our ___ love were but more faith - ful,

Are more ___ felt than up in ___ heaven; ___
We would ___ glad - ly trust God's ___ Word; ___

There is ___ no place where earth's fail - ings
And our ___ lives re - flect thanks - giv - ing

Have such ___ kind - ly ___ judg - ment ___ given.
For the ___ good - ness of ___ our ___ Lord.

THINE IS THE GLORY

words by
Edmond Louis Budry, 1884
Trans. R. Birch Hoyle, 1923

music by
Geroge Frideric Handel, 1748

1. Thine is the glo - ry,
2. Lo! Je - sus meets us,
3. No more we doubt Thee,

Ris - en, ___ con - quering Son;
Ris - en ___ from the tomb;
Glo - rious ___ Prince of life!

End - less ___ is the vic - tory,
Lov - ing - ly He greets us,
Life ___ is ___ nought with - out Thee,

Thou o'er death hast won.
Scat - ters fear and gloom.
Aid us in our strife.

An - gels ___ in bright rai - ment
Let ___ the ___ church with glad - ness
Make __ us __ more than con - querors

Rolled the stone a - way,
Hymns of tri - umph sing,
Through Thy death - less love;

Cm   F7

Kept	the	fold - ed	grave -	clothes
For	the	Lord now	liv -	eth;
Bring	us	safe through	Jor -	dan

Gm   Eb6   F7   Bb

Where	thy	bod - y	lay.
Death	hath	lost	its	sting.
To	Thy	home	a -	bove.

Refrain *(last time only)*
Eb

Thine   is   the   glo - ry,

Bb7   Eb Bb

Ris - en, __ con - quering Son;

Eb

End - less __ is the vic - tory

Fm   Eb6   Bbsus Bb7   Eb

Thou o'er death   hast won.

THIS IS MY FATHER'S WORLD

words by
Maltbie D. Babcock

music by
Franklin L. Sheppard

1. This is my Fa-ther's world, And to my lis-tening ears All na-ture sings, and round me rings The mu-sic of the spheres. This is my Fa-ther's world: I rest me in the thought Of rocks and trees, of skies and seas His hand the won-ders wrought.

2. This is my Fa-ther's world, The birds their car-ols raise, The morn-ing light, the lil-y white, De-clare their Mak-er's praise. This is my Fa-ther's world: He shines in all that's fair; In the rus-tling grass I hear Him pass, He speaks to me ev-ery-where.

3. This is my Fa-ther's world, O let me ne'er for-get That though the wrong seems oft so strong, God is the Rul-er yet. This is my Fa-ther's world: The bat-tle is not done; Je-sus who died shall be sat-is-fied, And earth and heav'n be one.

'TIS MIDNIGHT,
AND ON OLIVE'S BROW

words by
William B. Tappan, 1794–1849

music by
William B. Bradbury, 1816–1868

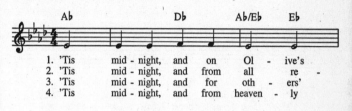

1. 'Tis mid-night, and on Ol - ive's
2. 'Tis mid-night, and from all re-
3. 'Tis mid-night, and for oth - ers'
4. 'Tis mid-night, and from heaven - ly

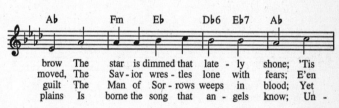

brow The star is dimmed that late - ly shone; 'Tis
moved, The Sav - ior wres - tles lone with fears; E'en
guilt The Man of Sor - rows weeps in blood; Yet
plains Is borne the song that an - gels know; Un -

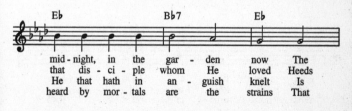

mid - night, in the gar - den now The
that dis - ci - ple whom He loved Heeds
He that hath in an - guish knelt Is
heard by mor - tals are the strains That

suf - fering Sav - ior prays a - lone.
not His Mas - ter's grief and tears.
not for - sak - en by His God.
sweet - ly soothe the Sav - ior's woe.

THIS JOYFUL EASTERTIDE

words by
George R. Woodward (1848–1934), alt.

music by
Vruechten, melody from
Psalmen, 1685
harm. Charles Wood (1866–1926)

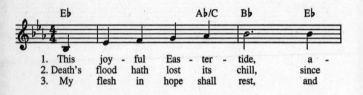

1. This joy-ful Eas-ter-tide, a-
2. Death's flood hath lost its chill, since
3. My flesh in hope shall rest, and

way with sin and sor - row! My
Je - sus crossed the riv - er: Lord
for a sea - son slum - ber, till

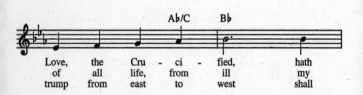

Love, the Cru-ci - fied, hath
of all life, from ill my
trump from east to west shall

Refrain

sprung to life this mor - row.
pass - ing life de - liv - er. Had
wake the dead in num - ber.

221

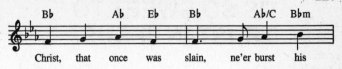

Christ, that once was slain, ne'er burst his

three - day pris - on, our

faith had been in vain; but

now is Christ a - ris - en, a -

ris - en, a - ris - en, a -

ris - en.

'TIS SO SWEET TO TRUST IN JESUS

words by
Louisa M.R. Stead

music by
William J. Kirkpatrick

1. 'Tis so sweet to trust in Je - sus,
2. O how sweet to trust in Je - sus,
3. Yes, 'tis sweet to trust in Je - sus,
4. I'm so glad I learned to trust Him,

Just to take Him at His word,
Just to trust His cleans-ing blood,
Just from sin and self to cease,
Pre - cious Je - sus, Sav - ior, Friend;

Just to rest up -
Just in sim - ple
Just from Je - sus
And I know that

on His prom - ise, Just to know "Thus saith the Lord."
faith to plunge me 'Neath the heal - ing, cleans-ing flood!
sim - ply tak - ing Life and rest and joy and peace.
He is with me, Will be with me to the end.

Refrain

Je - sus, Je - sus, how I trust Him!

How I've proved Him o'er and o'er! Je - sus, Je - sus,

pre - cious Je - sus! O for grace to trust Him more!

WE GATHER TOGETHER ²²³

words by
Netherlands folk hymn;
trans. by Theodore Baker

music by
Netherlands Folk song
arr. by Edward Kremser

1. We gath - er to - geth - er to ask the Lord's bless - ing; He chas - tens and has - tens His will to make known; The wick - ed op - press - ing now cease from dis - tress - ing, Sing prais - es to His name He for - gets not His own.

2. Be - side us to guide us, our God with us join - ing, Or - dain - ing, main - tain - ing His king - dom di - vine; So from the be - gin - ing the fight we were win - ning; Thou, Lord, wast at our side, all glo - ry be Thine!

3. We all do ex - tol Thee, Thou Lead - er tri - um - phant, And pray that Thou still our De - fend - er wilt be. Let Thy con - gre - ga - tion es - cape trib - u - la - tion: Thy name be ev - er praised! O Lord, make us free!

TO GOD BE THE GLORY

words by
Fanny J. Crosby (1823–1915)

music by
W.H. Doane (1832–1915)

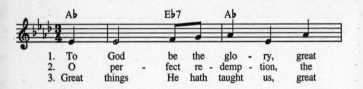

1. To God be the glo - ry, great
2. O per - fect re - demp - tion, the
3. Great things He hath taught us, great

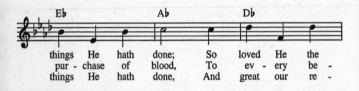

things He hath done; So loved He the
pur - chase of blood, To ev - ery be -
things He hath done, And great our re -

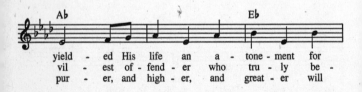

world that He gave us His Son, Who
liev - er the prom - ise of God; The
joic - ing through Je - sus the Son; But

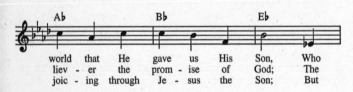

yield - ed His life an a - tone - ment for
vil - est of - fend - er who tru - ly be -
pur - er, and high - er, and great - er will

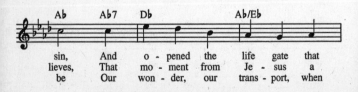

sin, And o - pened the life gate that
lieves, That mo - ment from Je - sus a
be Our won - der, our trans - port, when

225

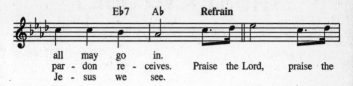

all may go in.
par - don re - ceives. Praise the Lord, praise the
Je - sus we see.

Lord, Let the earth hear His voice; Praise the

Lord, praise the Lord, Let the peo - ple re -

joice! O come to the Fa - ther, through

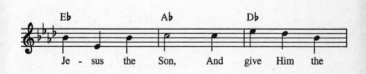

Je - sus the Son, And give Him the

glo - ry, great things He hath done.

226

TRUST AND OBEY

words by
John H. Sammis

music by
Daniel B. Towner

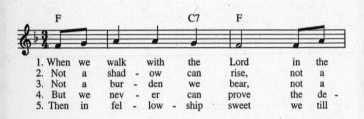

1. When we walk with the Lord in the
2. Not a shad - ow can rise, not a
3. Not a bur - den we bear, not a
4. But we nev - er can prove the de -
5. Then in fel - low - ship sweet we till

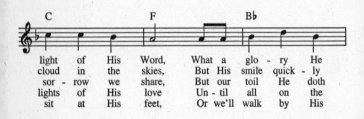

light of His Word, What a glo - ry He
cloud in the skies, But His smile quick - ly
sor - row we share, But our toil He doth
lights of His love Un - til all on the
sit at His feet, Or we'll walk by His

sheds on our way! While we do His good
drives it a - way; Not a doubt nor a
rich - ly re - pay; Not a grief nor a
al - tar we lay; For the fa - vor He
side in the way; What He says we will

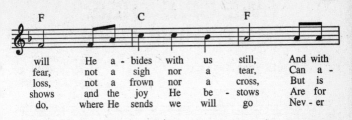

F		C		F	

will He a - bides with us still, And with
fear, not a sigh nor a tear, Can a -
loss, not a frown nor a cross, But is
shows and the joy He be - stows Are for
do, where He sends we will go Nev - er

Bb		F/C	C7	F

all who will trust and o - bey.
bide while we trust and o - bey.
blest if we trust and o - bey.
them who will trust and o - bey.
fear, on - ly trust and o - bey.

Refrain

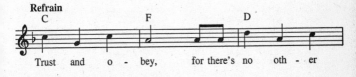

C	F	D

Trust and o - bey, for there's no oth - er

Gm	C7

way To be hap - py in

F	F/C	C7	F

Je - sus, But to trust and o - bey.

WE GIVE THEE BUT THINE OWN

words by
William W. How, 1823–1897, alt.

music by
Mason and Webb,
Cantica Lauda, 1850

1. We give thee but thine own, What e'er the gift my be; _____ All that we have is thine a - lone, A trust, O Lord, from thee.
2. May we thy boun - ties thus As stew - ards true re - ceive, _____ And glad - ly, as thou bless - est us, To thee our first - fruits give.
3. Hearts still are bruised and dead, And homes are bare and cold, _____ And lambs for whom the Shep - herd bled Are stray - ing from the fold.
4. To com - fort and to bless, To find a balm for woe, _____ To tend those lost in lone - li - ness, Is an - gels' work be - low.
5. The cap - tive to re - lease, The lost to God to bring, _____ To teach the way of life and peace, It is a Christ - like thing.
6. And we be - lieve Thy word, Though dim our faith may be; _____ What e'er we do for thine, O Lord, We do it un - to thee.

WE WOULD SEE JESUS

words by
Anna B. Warner

music by
Franklin E. Belden

1. "We would see Je - sus;" for the shad-ows length-en A - cross the lit - tle land-scape of our life; We would see Je - sus, our weak faith to strength - en For the last con - flict, in this mor - tal strife.

2. "We would see Je - sus;" Rock of our sal - va - tion, Where-on our feet were set with sov-'reign grace; Not life, nor death, __ with all their ag - i - ta - tion, Can thence re - move us, gaz - ing on His face.

3. "We would see Je - sus;" oth - er lights are pal - ing, Which for long years we did re - joice to see; The bless-ings of __ this sin - ful world are fail - ing; We would not plead - ing, Soon to re - mourn them, in ex - change for Thee.

4. "We would see Je - sus;" this is all we're need - ing Strength, joy, and will - ing - ness come with the sight; We would see Je - sus, dy - ing, ris - en, turn and end this mor - tal night!

230

WE PLOW THE FIELDS AND SCATTER

words by
Matthias Claudius, 1740–1815
tr. Jane M. Campbell, 1817–1878, alt.

music by
Johann A.P. Schulz, 1747–1800

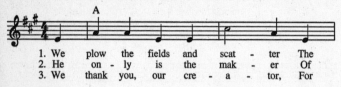

1. We plow the fields and scat - ter The
2. He on - ly is the mak - er Of
3. We thank you, our cre - a - tor, For

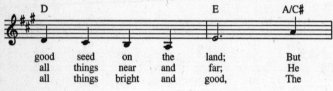

good seed on the land; But
all things near and far; He
all things bright and good, The

it is fed and wa - tered By
paints the way - side flow - er, He
seed - time and the har - vest, Our

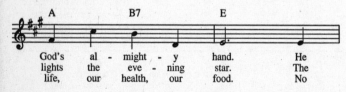

God's al - might - y hand. He
lights the eve - ning star. The
life, our health, our food. No

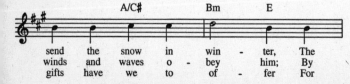

send the snow in win - ter, The
winds and waves o - bey him; By
gifts have we to of - fer For

231

WE'RE MARCHING TO ZION

words by
Isaac Watts

music by
Robert Lowry

1. Come, we that love the Lord, And
2. Let those re - fuse to sing Who
3. The hill of Zi - on yields A
4. Then let our songs a - bound, And

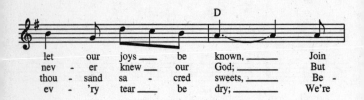

let our joys be known, Join
nev - er knew our God; But
thou - sand sa - cred sweets, Be -
ev - 'ry tear be dry; We're

in a song with sweet ac - cord, Join
chil - dren of the heav - 'nly King, But
fore we reach the heav - 'nly fields, Be -
march - ing thru Im - man - uel's ground, We're

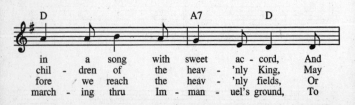

in a song with sweet ac - cord, And
chil - dren of the heav - 'nly King, May
fore we reach the heav - 'nly fields, Or
march - ing thru Im - man - uel's ground, To

233

thus sur - round the throne, And
speak their joys a - broad, May
walk the gold - en streets, Or
fair - er worlds on high, To

thus sur - round the throne. _____
speak their joys a - broad. _____
walk the gold - en streets. _____
fair - er worlds on high. _____

Refrain

We're

march - ing to Zi - on,

beau - ti - ful, beau - ti - ful Zi - on; We're

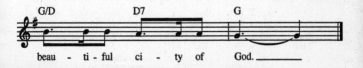

march - ing up - ward to Zi - on, _____ The

beau - ti - ful ci - ty of God. _____

WERE YOU THERE

words by
Afro-American spiritual

music by
Were You There, Afro-American spiritual
harm. Charles Winfred Douglas (1867-1944)

E   B7

1. Were you there when they cru - ci - fied my
2. Were you there when they nailed him to the
3. Were you there when they pierced him in the
4. Were you there when they laid him in the

E   C#m   E

Lord? Were you there when they cru - ci - fied my
tree? Were you there when they nailed him to the
side? Were you there when they pierced him in the
tomb? Were you there when they laid him in the

B   E   A   E

Lord?   Oh! _____
tree?   Oh! _____
side?   Oh! _____
tomb?   Oh! _____

A   E   G#/B#   C#m   A

Some - times it caus - es me to trem - ble,
Some - times it caus - es me to trem - ble,
Some - times it caus - es me to trem - ble,
Some - times it caus - es me to trem - ble,

B   A

trem - ble, trem - ble. Were you
trem - ble, trem - ble. Were you
trem - ble, trem - ble. Were you
trem - ble, trem - ble. Were you

E/B   B7   E

there when they cru - ci - fied my Lord?
there when they nailed him to the tree?
there when they pierced him in the side?
there when they laid him in the tomb?

WHAT A FRIEND
WE HAVE IN JESUS

words by
Joseph Scriven

music by
Charles C. Converse

1. What a friend we have in Je - sus, All our sins and griefs to
2. Have we trials _ and temp-ta - tions, Is there trou-ble an - y -
3. Are we weak and heav - y la - den, Cum-bered with a load of

bear. What a priv - i - lege to car - ry
where? We should nev - er be dis - cour - aged
care? Pre - cious Sav - ior still our ref - uge,

Ev - 'ry-thing to God in pray'r. O what peace we of - ten
Take it to the Lord in pray'r. Can we find a friend so
Take it to the Lord in pray'r. Do thy friends de-spise, for -

for - feit, O what need-less pain we bear,
faith - ful, Who will all our sor-rows share?
sake thee? Take it to the Lord in pray'r.

All be - cause we do not car - ry
Je - sus knows our ev - 'ry weak - ness,
In His arms He'll take and shield thee,

Ev - 'ry - thing to God in pray'r.
Take it to the Lord in pray'r.
Thou wilt find a sol - ace there.

WHAT WONDROUS LOVE IS THIS

words by
American Folk Hymn

music by
William Walker's *Southern Harmony*, 1835

1. What won-drous love is this, O my soul, O my soul! What won-drous love is this, O my soul! That caused the Lord of bliss To bear the dread-ful curse for my soul, for my soul, To bear the dread-ful curse for my soul.

2. When I was sink-ing down, sink-ing down, sink-ing down, When I was sink-ing down, sink-ing down, When I was sink-ing down Be-neath God's right-eous frown, Christ laid a-side His crown for my soul, for my soul, Christ laid a-side His crown for my soul.

3. To God and to the Lamb I will sing, I will sing, To God and to the Lamb I will sing, To God and to the Lamb Who is the great "I Am," While mil-lions join the theme, I will sing, I will sing, While mil-lions join the theme, I will sing.

4. And when from death I'm free, I'll sing on, I'll sing on, And when from death I'm free, I'll sing on, And when from death I'm free, I'll sing and joy-ful be, And thro' e-ter-ni-ty I'll sing on, I'll sing on, And thro' e-ter-ni-ty I'll sing on.

WHEN I SURVEY
THE WONDROUS CROSS

words by
Isaac Watts

music by
Based on a Gregorian chant
arr. Lowell Mason

1. When I sur - vey the _____
2. For - bid it, Lord, that _____
3. See, from His head, His _____
4. Were the whole realm of _____

won - drous _____ cross On which the
I should _____ boast, Save in the
hands, His _____ feet, Sor - row and
na - ture mine, That were a

Prince of _____ glo - ry _____ died,
death of _____ Christ, my _____ God;
love flow _____ min - gled _____ down;
pres - ent far too _____ small;

My rich - est gain I _____
All the vain things that _____
Did e'er such love and _____
Love so a - maz - ing,

count but _____ loss, And pour con -
charm me _____ most I sac - ri -
sor - row meet, Or thorns com -
so di - vine, De - mands my

tempt on all my _____ pride.
fice them to His _____ blood.
pose so rich a _____ crown?
soul, my life, my _____ all.

WHEN JESUS WEPT

words and music by
William Billings, 1770

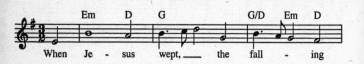

When Je - sus wept,___ the fall - ing

tear In mer - cy flowed ___ be -

yond all bound; When Je - sus

groaned, ___ a trem - bling fear Seized

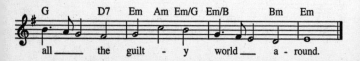

all ___ the guilt - y world ___ a - round.

WHEN MORNING GILDS THE SKIES

words by
Katholisches Gesangbuch, Würzburg, 1828
tr. by Edward Caswall

music by
Joseph Barnby

1. When morn-ing gilds the skies, _____ My heart a-wak-ing cries, May Je-sus Christ be praised! A-like at work and prayer To Je-sus I re-pair, May Je-sus Christ be praised!
2. The night be-comes as day, _____ When from the heart we say, May Je-sus Christ be praised! The pow'rs of dark-ness fear When this sweet chant they hear. May Je-sus Christ be praised!
3. Ye na-tions of man-kind, _____ In this your con-cord find, May Je-sus Christ be praised! Let all the earth a-round Ring joy-ous with the sound, May Je-sus Christ be praised!
4. Be this, while life is mine, _____ My can-ti-cle di-vine, May Je-sus Christ be praised! Be this th'e-ter-nal song Thro' all the a-ges long, May Je-sus Christ be praised!

WHEN THE ROLL IS CALLED UP YONDER

words by
James M. Black, 1856–1938

music by
James M. Black, 1856-1938

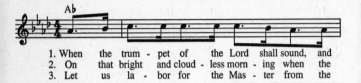

1. When the trum - pet of the Lord shall sound, and
2. On that bright and cloud - less morn - ing when the
3. Let us la - bor for the Mas - ter from the

time shall be no more, And the
dead in Christ shall rise, And the
dawn till set - ting sun, Let us

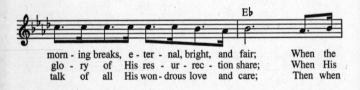

morn - ing breaks, e - ter - nal, bright, and fair; When the
glo - ry of His res - ur - rec - tion share; When His
talk of all His won - drous love and care; Then when

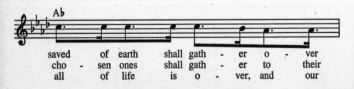

saved of earth shall gath - er o - ver
cho - sen ones shall gath - er to their
all of life is o - ver, and our

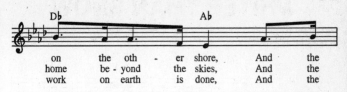

on the oth - er shore, And the
home be - yond the skies, And the
work on earth is done, And the

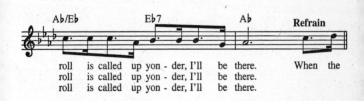

roll is called up yon - der, I'll be there. When the
roll is called up yon - der, I'll be there.
roll is called up yon - der, I'll be there.

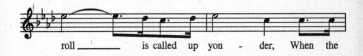

roll _____ is called up yon - der, When the

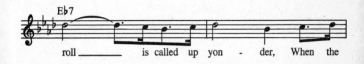

roll _____ is called up yon - der, When the

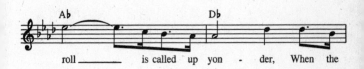

roll _____ is called up yon - der, When the

roll is called up yon - der, I'll be there.

242

WHITER THAN SNOW

words by
James Nicholson

music by
William G. Fischer

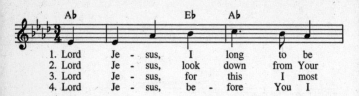

1. Lord Je - sus, I long to be
2. Lord Je - sus, look down from Your
3. Lord Je - sus, for this I most
4. Lord Je - sus, be - fore You I

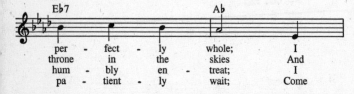

per - fect - ly whole; I
throne in the skies And
hum - bly en - treat; I
pa - tient - ly wait; Come

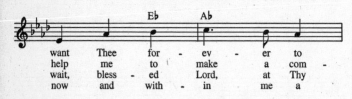

want Thee for - ev - er to
help me to make a com -
wait, bless - ed Lord, at Thy
now and with - in me a

live in my soul. Break
plete sac - ri - fice. I
cru - ci - fied feet. By
new heart cre - ate. To

down ev - ery i - dol, cast
give up my - self ___ and what -
faith, for my cleans - ing I
those who have sought ___ You, You

Ab

out	ev - ery	foe	Now
ev - er	I	know	Now
see	Your	blood	flow	Now
nev - er	said,	"No"	Now

Ab/Eb

wash	me	and	I	shall	be
wash	me	and	I	shall	be
wash	me	and	I	shall	be
wash	me	and	I	shall	be

Eb7   Ab

whit - er	than	snow.
whit - er	than	snow.
whit - er	than	snow.
whit - er	than	snow.

Refrain

Eb7   Fm

Whit - er than snow, yes,

Db   Ab   Db

whit - er than snow Now wash me and

Ab/Eb   Eb7   Ab

I shall be whit - er than snow.

WHO IS ON THE LORD'S SIDE?

words by
Frances Ridley Havergal

music by
C. Luise Reichardt
arr. by John Goss

1. Who is on the Lord's side?
2. Not for weight of glo - ry,
3. Je - sus, Thou hast bought us,
4. Fierce may be the con - flict,

Who will serve the King?
Not for crown and palm,
Not with gold or gem,
Strong may be the foe,

Who will be His help - ers,
En - ter we the ar - my,
But with Thine own life - blood,
But the King's own ar - my

Oth - er lives to bring?
Raise the war - rior psalm;
For Thy di - a - dem.
None can o - ver - throw.

Who will leave the world's side?
But for love that claim - eth
With Thy bless - ing fill - ing
Round His stand - ard rang - ing;

Bb/F   F

Who will face the foe?
Lives for whom He died;
Each who comes to Thee,
Vic - t'ry is se - cure;

Bb   F7/C   Bb/D   Eb

Who is on the Lord's side? Who for
He whom Je - sus nam - eth Must be
Thou hast made us will - ing, Thou hast
For His truth un - chang - ing Makes the

Bb/F   F7   Bb

Him will go? By Thy call of
on His side. By Thy love con -
made us free. By Thy grand re -
tri - umph sure. Joy - ful - ly en -

Eb   Bb

mer - cy, By Thy grace di -
strain - ing, By Thy grace di -
demp - tion, By Thy grace di -
list - ing By Thy grace di -

F   Gm   Eb

vine, We are on the
vine, We are on the
vine, We are on the
vine, We are on the

Bb   F7   Bb

Lord's side, Sav - ior, we are Thine.
Lord's side, Sav - ior, we are Thine.
Lord's side, Sav - ior, we are Thine.
Lord's side, Sav - ior, we are Thine.

WONDERFUL WORDS OF LIFE

words by
Philip P. Bliss

music by
Philip P. Bliss

1. Sing them o - ver a - gain to me,
2. Christ, the bless - ed One, gives to all
3. Sweet - ly ech - o the gos - pel call,

Won - der - ful words of Life; _____
Won - der - ful words of Life; _____
Won - der - ful words of Life; _____

Let me more of their beau - ty see,
Sin - ner, list to the lov - ing call,
Of - fer par - don and peace to all,

Won - der - ful words of Life. _____
Won - der - ful words of Life. _____
Won - der - ful words of Life. _____

Words of life _____ and beau - ty,
All so free - ly giv - en,
Je - sus, on - ly Sav - ior,

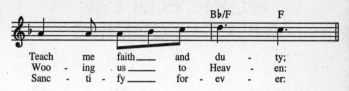

Teach me faith___ and du - ty;
Woo - ing us ___ to Heav - en:
Sanc - ti - fy ___ for - ev - er:

Refrain

Beau - ti - ful words, won - der - ful words,

Won - der - ful words of Life. _____

Beau - ti - ful words, won - der - ful words,

Won - der - ful words of Life. _____

WORK, FOR THE NIGHT IS COMING

words by
Annie L. Coghill, 1836–1907

music by
Lowell Mason, 1792–1872

1. Work, for the night is com - ing;
2. Work, for the night is com - ing;
3. Work, for the night is com - ing;

Work through the morn - ing hours; Work while the dew is
Work through the sun - ny noon; Fill bright - est hours with
Un - der the sun - set skies; While their bright tints are

spark - ling; Work mid spring - ing flowers;
la - bor; Rest comes sure and soon.
glow - ing, Work, for day - light flies.

Work when the day grows bright - er;
Give ev - ery fly - ing min - ute
Work till the last beam fad - eth,

Work in the glow - ing sun; Work, for the night is
Some - thing to keep in store; Work, for the night is
Fad - eth to shine no more; Work while the night is

com - ing, When man's work is done.
com - ing, When man works no more.
dark - ening, When man's work is o'er.

YE SERVANTS OF GOD

words by
Charles Wesley, 1744 (Rev. 7:9–12)

music by
Attr. to William Croft, 1708

1. Ye servants of God, your Master proclaim, and publish abroad his wonderful name; the name all-victorious of Jesus extol, his kingdom is glorious and rules over all.

2. God ruleth on high, almighty to save, and still he is nigh, his presence we have; the great congregation his triumph shall sing, ascribing salvation to Jesus, our King.

3. "Salvation to God, who sits on the throne!" Let all cry aloud and honor the Son; the praises of Jesus the angels proclaim, fall down on their faces and worship the Lamb.

4. Then let us adore and give him his right, all glory and power, all wisdom and might; all honor and blessing with angels above, and thanks never ceasing and infinite love.

YIELD NOT TO TEMPTATION

words by
Horatio R. Palmer, 1834–1907

music by
Horatio R. Palmer, 1834-1907

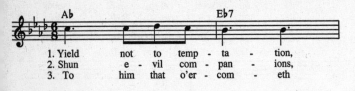

1. Yield not to temp - ta - tion,
2. Shun e - vil com - pan - ions,
3. To him that o'er - com - eth

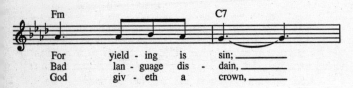

For yield - ing is sin;
Bad lan - guage dis - dain,
God giv - eth a crown,

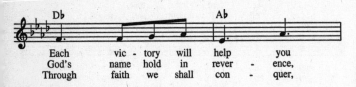

Each vic - tory will help you
God's name hold in rever - ence,
Through faith we shall con - quer,

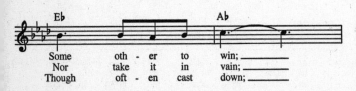

Some oth - er to win;
Nor take it in vain;
Though oft - en cast down;

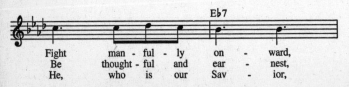

Fight man - ful - ly on - ward,
Be thought - ful and ear - nest,
He, who is our Sav - ior,

Fm · · · · · C7

Dark pas - sions sub - due; _____
Kind - heart - ed and true; _____
Our strength will re - new; _____

Db · · · · Ab

Look ev - er to Je - sus,
Look ev - er to Je - sus,
Look ev - er to Je - sus,

Eb7 · · · · Ab

He'll car - ry you through. _____
He'll car - ry you through. _____
He'll car - ry you through. _____

Refrain

Ask the Sav - ior to help you,

Eb · · · Ab

Com - fort, strength - en, and keep you;

Db · · · · Ab

He is will - ing to aid you,

Eb7 · · · · Ab

He will car - ry you through. _____

GUITAR CHORD FRAMES

	C	Cm	C+	C6	Cm6
C					

	C#	C#m	C#+	C#6	C#m6
C#/Db					

	D	Dm	D+	D6	Dm6
D					

	Eb	Ebm	Eb+	Eb6	Ebm6
Eb/D#					

	E	Em	E+	E6	Em6
E					

	F	Fm	F+	F6	Fm6
F					

This guitar chord reference includes 120 commonly used chords. For a more complete guide to guitar chords, see "THE PAPERBACK CHORD BOOK" (HL00702009).

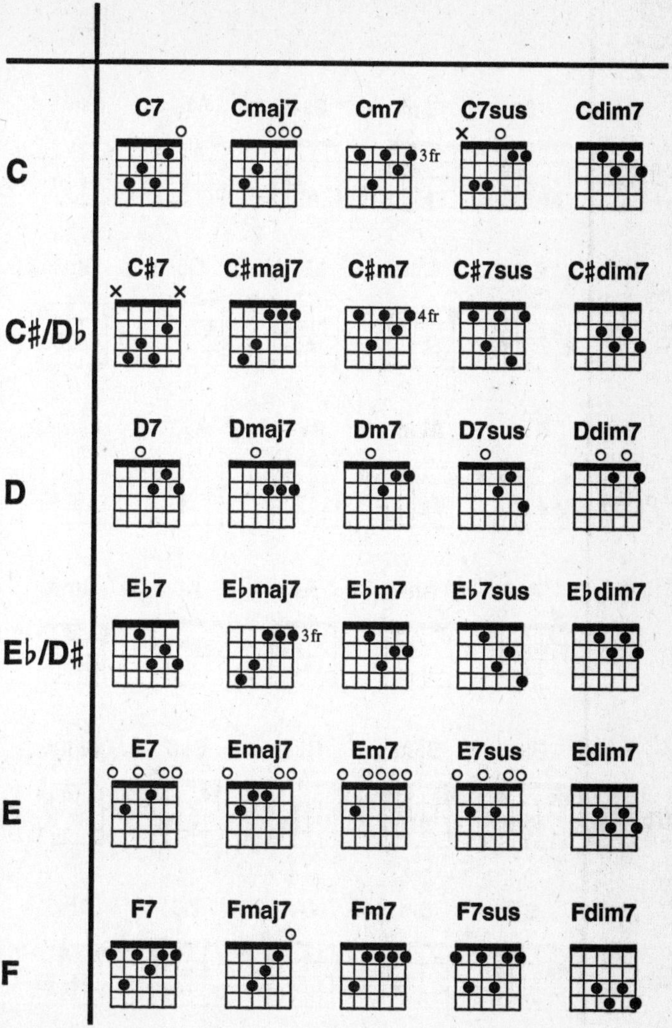
C
C7
Cmaj7
Cm7
3fr
C7sus
Cdim7
C♯/D♭
C♯7
C♯maj7
C♯m7
4fr
C♯7sus
C♯dim7
D
D7
Dmaj7
Dm7
D7sus
Ddim7
E♭/D♯
E♭7
E♭maj7
3fr
E♭m7
E♭7sus
E♭dim7
E
E7
Emaj7
Em7
E7sus
Edim7
F
F7
Fmaj7
Fm7
F7sus
Fdim7

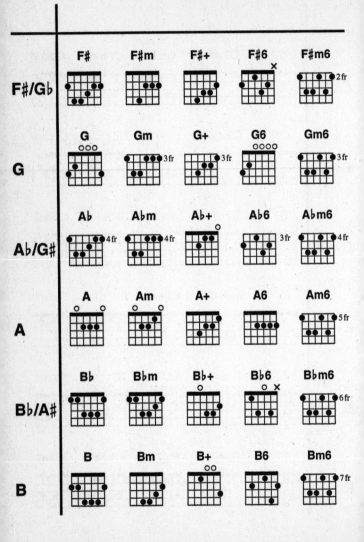

	F#7	F#maj7	F#m7	F#7sus	F#dim7
F#/Gb					

	G7	Gmaj7	Gm7	G7sus	Gdim7
G					

	Ab7	Abmaj7	Abm7	Ab7sus	Abdim7
Ab/G#					

	A7	Amaj7	Am7	A7sus	Adim7
A					

	Bb7	Bbmaj7	Bbm7	Bb7sus	Bbdim7
Bb/A#					

	B7	Bmaj7	Bm7	B7sus	Bdim7
B					

THE PAPERBACK SONGS SERIES

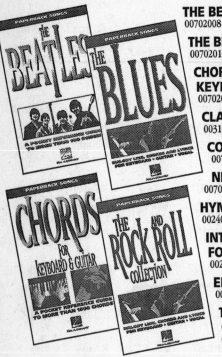